RUSTY AND I

'Swapan K. Banerjee is the ideal interviewer . . . He is a Boswell of sorts, a Boswell not just to one writer—such as a Dr Johnson—but to many men of letters, musicians and others . . . Indian writing needs more Boswell of the Swapan K. Banerjee kind.'

—Ruskin Bond

'. . . have the knack of elicitating the deeper layers of a writer's urges. Commendable for the readers but a bit scary for the writer! You deserve a diploma in forensic science.'

—Bill Aitken (renowned Indian travel writer)

RUSTY AND I

UP-CLOSE WITH RUSKIN BOND

Swapan K. Banerjee

Introduction by
Manoj Das

Rupa . Co

Published 2009 by

Rupa . Co

7/16, Ansari Road, Daryaganj
New Delhi 110 002

Sales Centres:

Allahabad Bangalooru Chandigarh Chennai
Hyderabad Jaipur Kathmandu
Kolkata Mumbai

Typeset by
Mindways Design
1410 Chiranjiv Tower
43 Nehru Place
New Delhi 110 019

Printed in India by
Nutech Photolithographers
B-240, Okhla Industrial Area, Phase-I,
New Delhi 110 020, India

Contents

Acknowledgement

Due thanks to the following copyright owners and publishers for publishing some of the pieces on Ruskin Bond included in this volume: *The Statesman, The Times of India, The Economic Times, The Asian Age, The Himachal Times, Indo-Asian Literature* and *Garhwal Post.*

Some articles appeared in the newspapers/magazines that have since closed down. These include: *Amrita Bazar Patrika, Brown Critique*, *Scoria,* and *Scholar World.*

Introduction

As I begin writing this introduction to Swapan K. Banerjee's fascinating work, I wake up to the fact that I am celebrating the fortieth year of my meeting with Ruskin Bond.

The Mussoorie of 1968 had a reticent face and in winter it had grown as introvert as its prize dweller Ruskin Bond, who was then living in a log cabin called Maplewood Lodge that looked lost in trance in a setting dominated by meditative trees and luxuriant and blossoming bushes sloping around. (The bungalow's solitude was not without its sadder aspect: Ruskin's lovely dog had been taken away by a leopard a few days earlier.)

From Delhi through Roorkee, moving towards Haridwar and taking a diversion to have a glimpse of Rishikesh, the drive was thrilling for a first timer. The prospect of meeting Ruskin Bond at its termination made it unforgettable; a memory that brings the good old nostalgic poet William Cowper to mind:

What peaceful hours I once enjoyed!
How sweet their memory still!
But they have left an aching void,
The world can never fill.

A chilly evening was setting in when I stood in front of Bond's solitary lodge, a suave and gracious young man greeting me and speaking with unmistakable joy, 'Uncle was expecting you any moment; well there he is!'

There he was, climbing fast up a slope through rows of trees in the company of a Punjabi friend who was related to Ruskin in some way. Ruskin and I were of the same age. But during that meeting forty years ago, none of us showed any sign of age and within a few minutes, we were talking and laughing like two boys who had been playmates since the 'moment zero' of their lives. He had written to me earlier that I must not plan putting myself up anywhere else. Now he and the young man were busy arranging a cosy bed in a room on the ground floor for my driver. The shy driver looked at me and murmured that he could make himself quite comfortable in the car itself, to which Ruskin's rejoinder was, 'And comfortably frozen by dawn!'

That was the instant human Bond, a value that pervades his works. That does not become evident in case of all the writers. The great values that some of their works exude, cannot necessarily be traced in their makers.

By the time we were out for a walk on the narrow zigzag road carved out of the hill's surface, a chunk of sky seemed to have fallen on the valley below where we could see thousands of lights mimicking the stars above. We had our dinner in a roadside restaurant, this author trying to assimilate as mundane an activity as eating with the infinity spread outside the window, a process in which Ruskin had probably achieved his *siddhi*.

We did talk of mice and men long into the night. Ruskin was reminiscing how, once in a while, he would toy with the idea of taking up a job if at all that was possible. But the very next day, a cheque would arrive from a magazine or a publisher inscribing an amount that would be a pittance when compared to what he receives today, but enough to triumphantly reject the gloomy prospect of any alternative to writing.

Soon after I returned to Pondicherry (Now Puducherry), I read a piece in *The Statesman*, entitled 'Of Human Bondage'. It began

'Bond is dying'. The rest was an account of the author meeting Ruskin when the writer was ill and the nostalgia was carried to such an extreme that I sat shocked and silent, wondering if I had missed an earlier obituary! I asked a distinguished friend to read the article and tell me what it conveys. He read it attentively. 'Obviously your friend, already a recluse, has finally retired from life!' was his comment.

Oh no! I sent a reply-paid telegram to the principal of a school in the neighbourhood of Maplewood Lodge, whom I had met while strolling with Ruskin, requesting him to let me know how my friend fared. To my great relief, the reply came from an amused Ruskin.

Both of us were writing for people from different age groups, both grown-ups and children. The inimitable cartoonist Mario Miranda illustrated Ruskin's *The Grandfather's Private Zoo* and *Stories of Light and Delight* by me. Both did very well. Ruskin had the uncanny gift of making many of his children's stories memorable for adults. Even then, despite his having received the John Llewellyn Rhys Prize at that stage of his life, Ruskin Bond—the name itself as inviting as a gem to be picked up today—needed a legend on the cover of his book, even if of uncertain merit. In the mid-sixties of the last century, Higginbothams, the famous chain of book sellers and distributors spread over the Southern Railway stations with headquarters at Chennai (then Madras), launched itself into publishing. Among their very first releases was a book by Ruskin, *The Neighbour's Wife and Other Stories* and one by me, *A Song for Sunday and Other Stories*. Ruskin's book had come through some literary agent trying out the prospect in India, and he had put on the cover 'A Book Club Award Winner'. Ruskin wrote to me asking if I had any knowledge of what that announcement meant. Well, it must have been a club consisting of the hopeful agent and his partner, his life-partner if he had no business partner I presumed.

The situation began to change, fast or slow is a relative matter, and one day Ruskin wrote to me that he had just been entrusted with the editorship of *Imprint* and he expected me to write for it more frequently than I did till then. It was one of the happiest news related to my literary world I had ever received. Many readers would not know its significance today. *Imprint*, once founded by Phillip Knightley (later a senior editor of *The Sunday Times*, London) and his friends, was the most prestigious English magazine in those days, next in circulation only to *The Illustrated Weekly of India*. It had been taken over by the group owned by Mr R.V. Pandit, who published it from Hong Kong before shifting to Bombay (now Mumbai). The news magazines have devoured all such literary and semi-literary publications, making it more and more difficult for creative writers to prove their talent. To be published in *The Illustrated Weekly* and *Imprint* amounted to standing. I was so happy primarily because with a connoisseur like Ruskin as its editor, the magazine could now bring to the forefront more and more talented writers in need of recognition. Another reason for my happiness was my knowledge that Mr Pandit was generous in payment and the assignment would surely free Ruskin from some worries. And before long I was amused to hear from him, 'Gone are the good days when one was not bothered about income tax. . . !'

Around that time he had been charged with obscenity in a novelette, serialised in an avant-garde Bombay monthly, as mentioned in an interview with him in this volume. He wrote to me saying that his lawyer had advised him to find a writer or writers, having some credentials, to declare in the court that the accusation was wrong from the literary point of view. Although Ruskin was far better known by then, he had not received the Sahitya Akademi award whereas I had got it.

Ruskin also informed me the date on which the case was to come up in a Bombay court. I had an invitation from the University of Bombay to give a series of talks under an endowment. Too willing to come to Ruskin's defence, I requested the University authorities to shift my talks to dates nearer the hearing of the case and they obliged. But the case was shifted to another date. Since it would be difficult for me to tarry there and there were chances of a shift in the date again, as I was told by the editor who was the co-accused, I decided to request some eminent writers to rally to Ruskin's defence. The first one I approached was an influential journalist. 'Have you read the controversial novelette?' he asked me gravely. Alas, I had not and I said so. 'It is indefensible,' he observed, agitated. 'Indefensible? Ruskin cannot write any indefensible stuff,' I asserted. He calmed down. 'Once in a while he can, and perhaps any author can. The editor can demand of a writer a piece that suits the character of his journal; the author may be in dire need of money – more so if the latter depends entirely on earning from his writing and Mr Bond, as I gather, does so. My advice is, you read the novelette before defending it.'

'Thanks. But I believe that there are people who are greater than their deeds. Even if Ruskin would have written anything that was objectionable according to you or a court of law, it may not be really objectionable in a wider perspective. And if I too found it objectionable, I will conclude that the author—he being Ruskin Bond—had only temporarily strayed out of his *swadharma* – his path of tender sunlight with wondrous Himalayan flowers on both the sides capable of offering their fragrance to readers thousands of miles away,' I said and then I met Shri Nissin Ezekiel and Shri Khushwant Singh in their professorial and editorial office respectively. Both of them instantly gave their consent to appear in the court whenever warranted. Ruskin was very dear to them.

Years have rolled by and I have forgotten whether the case against Ruskin failed or was withdrawn, but I was informed that these eminent writers kept their promise.

Ruskin became my prize contributor when I edited *The Heritage* (1985-89), the first issue carrying one of his famous stories, *The Cricket Fever*. Our names appear in the English edition of *Chandamama*, the largest circulated children's magazine in the country, as editorial advisers but we are able to meet only on rare occasions. One such event was the World Book Fair held in New Delhi a few years ago. He gave the inaugural lecture and I delivered the key-note address there. That was an occasion when we had plenty of opportunities to talk as we were put up in the same guesthouse – India International Centre. It was only then that I realised what a witty conversationalist he is. I am privileged to enjoy it over the phone from time to time, his voice bringing to me at the southern shores the vibrations of the enchanting valley into which his window opens.

I paid brief visits to him twice during the past decade. I was led by my host at Dehradun, Shri Surjit Kishore Das who is the chief secretary of the Government of Uttaranchal, himself a gifted writer and held in affection by Ruskin. (I should recommend to the readers Surjit Babu's *The Queen is Dying*, an excellent work of fiction on the tragedy of the hills of Mussoorie. But the work, I am afraid, is not available now.) If Ruskin was a challenge to all of us for using nothing more than a manual typewriter in this era, on the second visit I found out that he had given up even that; he submitted handwritten manuscripts to publishers—a daring stance that only he could take.

Swapan K. Banerjee's is a work with a difference; though basically a human approach to the subject, it is well-provided with scholastic penetrations into Ruskin's works. But its speciality lies in its variety: studies, interviews, reviews and reminiscences.

By the time one finishes reading it, the impression that lingers is absolutely in keeping with the literary personality of Ruskin. Banerjee himself has put it beautifully: 'Reading a Bond story is like watching a glorious sunset. The story, like the sunset, fades out. But what is experienced is preserved in the store of the reader's memory forever.'

Banerjee's work, a decent and distinct tribute to Ruskin Bond, deserves a response at the same wave-length – one of love.

Manoj Das

Rendezvous with Rusty

I read the story 'The Woman on Platform 8' in the late eighties, when a friend of mine gifted me the short story collection *The Night Train at Deoli and Other Stories*. Since then, I have been on a hunting spree for other books by the same author—at the library, at the bookshop, at the station stall . . . everywhere.

Never did I imagine then that one day I would do an article on his heart-tugging love stories, and it would also see the light of day!

That was to be the nineteenth article of my hack-writing career. As I held the pen, a mass of ideas, echoes of other great writers, avalanched upon me. How I struggled during the course of preparing the synopses of the stories chosen for the write-up. And then I had to pit his cameos against those of other masters with whom he has such strong spiritual affinity.

I did my best of course and sent the article to a very-well-known-but-now-defunct daily (*Amrita Bazar Patrika*) where I had contributed before.

One memorable May morning, it did appear in the daily. With some trepidation I sent my favourite author a copy, asking for his express permission for a heart-to-heart exchange. To my pleasant surprise, he wrote back with the kind comments: 'Your article on my love stories is a perceptive and finely-written piece. . . .'

As the interview at his cosy cottage perched on the crest of a hill in Mussoorie some time back was drawing to a close,

Ruskin Bond told me in his professorial voice, as inimitable as his style of writing:

'I sent your article to Boston University. They have started an archive. They have, what you call, a special collection on different writers. They asked me if I'd give them some of my papers, reviews . . . I included your piece. It's now enshrined in. . . .'

I could not believe my ears. I became, for a few moments, tongue-tied from too much to verbalise. It was not exactly the honour of having one's article in the Boston University archive being looked after by the director, Dr Howard Gotlieb, but the fact that Mr Bond, 'one of the big guns in the writer's pantheon', had actually gone through it and liked it, made me fall to dwelling upon the possibility that perhaps there's a writer in me too!

On my way out, I again felt a tug at my tear-duct when he asked me to feel free to ask for anything including money if I happened to run into trouble during my stay in Mussoorie. 'You have my phone number, don't you?' He wanted to make sure. I folded my hands and bowed in utter reverence before taking leave of him.

(First published in *The Times of India*)

Reviews

Love is a Sad Song

'The art insists', says T.S. Eliot, 'that a man shall dispose of all that he has even of his family tree, and follow art alone.' Lifelong commitment to some form of art, for an artist worth his salt, is the only thing, uppermost in his mind, under the sun. Name any artist par excellence, and there is the saga of his supreme sacrifice that has gone into making the artist what he is. Ruskin Bond had only one dream in his childhood – to be a writer. When some people, thoroughly uninspired, with no commitment whatsoever to anything, tried their best to tempt and lure him away form the only path marked out for him, Bond's heart-out quip was always the same: I'd rather be a bad writer than be a successful businessman.

Over the years, Bond has written stories that speak volumes of the extraordinary depth and perception of his realisation with regard to 'link and boblink' in the game of life. He has crafted stories of myriad hues. But he excels, particularly, in writing love stories that never sink without a ripple.

Bond, in his childhood, for reasons a bit shrouded with mystery, cut away from his roots. His English mother Edith (Clerk) Bond, 'had gone away', when Ruskin was a four-year-old boy, nobody knew where. For a time Bond had no food to have his fill. He just 'blundered about' the strange, unknown places, absolutely unfellowed. Bond fashioned, when he was just seventeen, those days of acute distress into a novel – *The Room on the Roof.* This

John Llewellyn Rhys Prize-winning book is still widely read all over the world.

Rusty, the protagonist in *The Room on the Roof*, feels somewhat secure, financially, when he is appointed the teacher of Kishen, a schoolboy. Before long, he falls headlong in love with Kishen's 'mummy' Meena. Having been starved of warmth for a long time, he feels swept off his feet with blind love for Meena who, unhappy over her love marriage with Mr Kapoor, responds warmly. Young Rusty 'wanted to run away with Meena, into the hills, into the forest, where none could find them, and he wanted to be with her forever'.

Then Meena goes to Delhi in search of a suitable job for her husband (or for some other unknown reasons as Kapoor remarries immediately after Meena's mysterious death), never to return. The news of Meena's death comes like a shell that smashes Rusty's tender heart. Death snatches away the only person he once felt at home with, gave his heart outright to. Smitten with remorse, Rusty laments inconsolably: 'there will still be sun and litchis, and there will be other friends, but there will be no Meena.'

To get rid of the continuous twinge of insufferable grief, Rusty, one night, almost drinks himself to death while the image of Meena pops up whatever direction he looks in. But the writer in him rises superior to his flesh-and-blood grief. He ultimately snaps out of his dreadfully painful mood. 'I am not interested in today, I want tomorrow . . . I have to break away. I want to be either somebody or nobody. I don't want to be anybody.' It is really amazing how a seventeen-year-old boy could see into the life of things with such penetrating insight into the depths of human nature, and find the exact words to match his poetic feeling.

Bond's ability to express the intensity of Rusty's grief over the death of his beloved equals that of Turgenev in his *First Love* where the hero's bleeding heart, after the sudden death of his heart-throb, cries out bitterly for sense in an ephemeral world chockful of uncertainty, absurdity, and bewilderment.

In the introduction to his *The Night Train at Deoli and Other Stories*, Bond says: 'Well, that's it. I am fifty-four now. No more love stories, and no more falling in love . . . But then, on my way home, walking through the streets . . . I met this girl with the most beautiful smile in the world . . . But I'll tell about it another time.'

Bond has dedicated some of his poems and stories to one elusive Binya as Sunil Gangopadhyay has done to Neera, and Jibanananda Das to Banalata Sen. A collection of his stories, *Our Trees Still Grow in Dehra,* that has fetched him the coveted Sahitya Akademi Award, contains the story 'Binya Passes By'.

The protagonist in the story, while striking into an unfrequented pine-lined track, stops dead as a dulcet voice singing a song drips into his ears. His sudden rush of desire to meet the singer in the undulating range of mountains proves futile. But when at last he runs into her, he cannot bring himself to believe that a girl of 'fifteen-sixteen', of so simple and so rugged an appearance, can sing so beautifully. When he accepts a few bell berries from her, and her soft fingers touch his in the process, the smouldering feeling goes haywire. But the girl, after passing a few intimate moments with him, suddenly vanishes into thin air, leaving the hero in utter despair. At the end the hero broods, 'It isn't time that's passing by, it's you and I, it's you and I.'

The story is free from any message or moral and 'fades out like life' itself. Bond here helps the reader visualise, through word-painting, the whole landscape of the Garhwal region where 'mountains of silence and gentle reserve of shepherds and woodmen know me as one who walks among trees'.

It is interesting to note [that] 'Euterpe', a poem by Alfred Noyes, is somewhat similar, content-wise, to the story 'Binya

Passes By'. The following verse from the poem says it all, in a poetic garb though:

> 'The witchery of her voice from far blue hills
> At sunset, called me on
> With exquisite echoes of all those bird-like rills
> That warbles in helicon
> Once, over a cloud of thyme, I saw her gleam
> I touched her sunny side.
> She vanished, into the dusk, a moth-like dream.
> And all that music died.'

'Love is a Sad Song', another story included in the *Night Train at Deoli and Other Stories*, is monologic in nature. Here, the protagonist falls in love with the niece of his friend Dinesh when she visits his home nestled in the lap of mountains. An oppressive passion towards Sushila, a schoolgirl half his age, entwines his heart. Time skips by. The romance takes root. At the dead of night, when everybody falls fast asleep, they make love. Sometimes they go down to a stream. He takes bath with his beloved holding on to her 'like a clinging vine'.

Dinesh goes back to Delhi after the vacation, taking Sushila away from him. So the hero pines away with the sole question nibbling at his heart: 'If I could not pass a few weeks without you, how was I to pass a year, two years?' All his attempts to tie the knot fail miserably, particularly when a bank officer armed with a car enters the fray. Bond ends the story superbly: 'I may stop loving you, Sushila, but I will never stop loving the days I loved you'.

The way Bond articulates the stifling, maddening passion in a style embellished with neither rhetoric nor prolixity, deserves a comparison with the writing of Turgenev, once again. In *First Love* by Turgenev, the heroine Zinaida asks the hero to 'Jump down [from a fourteen-foot wall] if you really love me'. The hero, risking his very life, does her bidding without any hesitation whatsoever. Similarly, in 'Love is a Sad Song', when the protagonist asks Sushila not to 'crush' a butterfly she says:

If I spare it, what will you do for me. What will you pay?

Why, anything you say?

And will you kiss my foot?

Both feet, I said and did so willingly.

L'amour (French for love), in its very nature, is mysterious; something inexplicable. When it comes it is in a flash, without any intimation whatsoever. And once it enters someone, he is in for a shock, pleasant or otherwise, the reverberation of which never really ceases. In 'Time Stops at Shamli', a sequel to 'Love is a Sad Song', the protagonist on his way to Saharanpur, makes an unscheduled stop at Shamli, and in a 'correlated pattern of the game' meets his old flame Sushila, now married: 'Looking up at her again the only yearning . . . returned.'

Sheer physical attraction tugs both of them dangerously close to each other. But Sushila comes to her senses: 'What happiness would we have living in hiding from everyone we once knew and cared for?' The matter does not end here. The hero leaves Shamli disappointed, but not before letting us have a peep into his burning heart. At the end he says: 'Shamli would always be there. And I could always come back.'

The situational open-ended nature of the story invariably brings to mind 'The Lady with the Dog', a masterpiece by Anton Chekhov, where Gaurav and Anna, despite the nagging fear of their extra-marital infatuation being exposed to society, feel driven toward each other by every heave of their pulse. Every scheme to stay apart from each other fizzles out.

The story, as in life, ends without any permanent solution in sight, with the words, 'the most complicated part was only just beginning'. Bond's visual details too, like Chekhov's, are vivid and exact.

Bond expresses the problems of the human heart in conflict with itself, born out of both requited and unrequited love, with an absolute naturalness. He has in him the mood making genius of Argentinian writer Jorge Luis Borges, and a crystalline clarity such as Maugham had. His using first person narrative to express his own, and not vicarious experience, leaves a lingering impact upon the mind of the reader.

'Let no man', Bond urges all would-be artistes, 'take your dream away. It will sustain you to the end.' Today, Bond is indisputably one of the greatest short story writers in the world; but as a businessman, the less said about him the better, for the art of writing still remains his primary concern while he continues to ignore, like all great artistes, the value of his genius in monetary terms. The result is that he is deprived, more often than not, of what he so rightly deserves.

It is the glow of creation and the feel of spiritual release that helps him ignore all other *joie de vivre.*

(First published in *Amrita Bazar Patrika*)

The Romance and Mystery of Indian Railways

The doleful whistle and the moan of the train, as it streaks onward, the staccato rhythm of its clickety-clack, the view of the heaving hills or of the monotonous stretch of barren ground that flashes past the window alternately, never fail to affect the creative and sensitive people.

A train 'singing through the forest', or 'wheezing through mountain' always hooked John Godfray Saxe. To Thomas Wolfe, the thunder of the super fast express going westward in the dark was more than a memorable dream.

For Vladimir Nabokov it was the long-drawn sigh of a train coming to a halt that always set his imagination afire. But what affected him most were the lights in the distance, raking the sky that he never felt tired of watching through the window of a train in motion. He described those slipping lights as 'diamonds that I later gave away to my characters to alleviate the burden of my wealth'.

Ruskin Bond, the gifted Anglo-Indian writer, has also woven the romance and the mystery of railway platforms, compartments, and tracks in his haunting Indian railway stories. In the introduction to the *Penguin Book of Indian Railway Stories* he writes:

'. . . I love railway platforms. I spent a great deal of time on them when I was a boy, waiting for connecting trains to Kalka or

Saharanpur or Barrackpore or Rajkot. The odd incident stayed in my memory and when, in my late teens, I started writing short stories, these memories became stories. . . .'

In his 'Kipling's Simla', Bond expresses his pure feeling more eloquently:

'Small wayside stations have always fascinated me. Manned sometimes by just one or two men, and often situated in the middle of a damp sub-tropical forest, or clinging to the mountainside on the way to Simla or Darjeeling, these little stations are for me outposts of romance.'

Stretch of railway tracks—tortuous, running through mountainous terrain, to the point of the blue haze, springing mysteriously at places, out of a leafy grove—always fascinated Bond. During his childhood he used to watch, like Durga and Apu in *Pather Panchali* (a Bengali novel by Bibhutibhushan Bandyopadhyay), a charging engine spewing out clouds of white smoke and belching reddish sparks occasionally, entering a tunnel with a deafening roar and then smoothly moving out of it, till it disappeared, leaving behind a strange echo of its thundering cadence.

But crossing the track on foot was a terror to Bond. He was afraid of getting run over, for his strength always deserted him and his legs gave way whenever he came too close to the track.

In *The Adventures of Rusty,* he narrated his nightmare thus: 'I have always had a superstitious dread of crossing railway lines; I get a nightmare in which I find myself lying helpless (though not bound) on a railway track, while a steam engine thunders towards me. I've always woken up with the engine about three feet away, but some times I wonder what would happen if I failed to wake up at the last moment.'

Through his story 'The Woman on Platform 8', Bond has found the objective correlative of this nightmare.

In the story, the child protagonist Arun waits all alone at Ambala station for the connecting train to take him to his boarding school at Simla. Every time a train pulls in, he is caught in a 'an inferno of heaving, shouting, agitated human bodies', that sweep him much against his will, 'outside the station'. As he, tired of this game, sits on his suitcase and stares at the tracks stretched before him, a woman, a stranger, gets into a conversation with him. Though initially suspicious, Arun gradually grows intimate with her, and accompanies her to the railway canteen where he has his fill while answering her questions dipped in affection.

As they stride out of the canteen, the lady suddenly stops dead, her fingers digging deep into Arun's soft wrist. Arun swivels his head and watches a boy jumping off the platform on to the track. The boy clambers safely onto the other platform. Her grip slowly loosens, and they walk back to the place where Arun's suitcase is kept.

There Arun meets his friend Satish and his mother. When Satish's mother asks Arun about his mother, this lady, much to Arun's surprise, chimes, 'Yes, I am Arun's mother'. The train arrives. They occupy the window-side seats. Satish's mother runs off at the mouth; but this lady remains silent. Her eyes do the talking instead. As the whistle rings out, Arun 'leaned out of the window then, and put my lips to her cheek, and kissed her . . . she was looking at me as the train took me away . . . and I watched her until she was lost in the milling crowd'.

Bond's mother separated from his father when he was only four. 'Nothing my father said could bring my mother home; she had gone with another (Mr Harrison).' The lady in the story resembles the aunt his father stayed with after the divorce to a great extent.

Bond once did visit her house to see whether his father—who died when Bond was only ten—had left anything for him. And he liked his aunt who took good care of him. Her age, look and even the colour of the saree wrapped around her body as described in *The Adventures of Rusty* is no different from this mysterious lady character in the story.

Bond, through this timeless story, has laid to rest his terror of crossing the track, and also of the acute sense of loneliness of his affection-starved childhood.

In another railway story by Bond, 'The Eyes Have It', the protagonist is going to Dehra on his way to Mussoorie. He is blind, sitting alone in a certain compartment, only passing lights and shadows making impressions on his sightless senses. A lady boards the same compartment and sits across him, just hand-shaking distance away. Sick of being alone, he makes the first move, cautious that the fact of his being blind remains under wraps.

He dwells on the spirit-soaring weather in Dehra in October and on the interestingly pretty face of his co-passenger (he guesses it). But he, in this toughest 'game of chess', makes a wrong move to the point of committing a blunder when he asks, 'What is it like outside?' There is a moment of silence and then he heaves a sigh of relief as the lady apparently fails to grasp his helpless situation and counters, 'Why don't you look out of the window?'

Saharanpur arrives. The lady bids adieu, her dress almost caressing him, and disembarks. Another person, this time a gentleman, comes in her place and praises unreservedly the beauty of her eyes, adding, ruefully, 'but they were of no use to her. She was completely blind. Didn't you notice?'

'The Eyes Have It' demands just a few minutes, as each impeccably-crafted story by Bond generally does, but its impact upon the reader's mind is huge. The telling last line makes your heart miss a few beats as no reader can guess the fact of the beautiful lady being stark blind like her co-passenger by any stretch of the imagination, unless he happens to be Boccaccio.

Bond's Flaubert-like ability to mutate into the character he creates is vindicated strongly when the blind man in the story moves us by his desperate efforts to hide his terrible handicap.

The dialogues are crisp, conversational, and daring, almost taking you to the edge of the painful revelation, but never really spilling the beans, and thus keeping the reader on his tenterhooks, until the very end.

During a few hours of the train journey, a few moments are caught, shaped, and made still.

During the summer vacation, while travelling to his grandma's place at Dehra from his college, the station that particularly fascinated Bond was Deoli. This lonely, cute platform took his fancy, and he stepped out onto the platform one cold morning, overcome by the desire to talk to a rustic girl (in 'The Night Train at Deoli').

When pestered, he bought a basket; but before he could open his heart the bell clanged, forcing him to tear himself away from this girl. This brief brush with a young girl with 'dark smouldering eyes' bowled him over.

Two months later, as he was passing by the same route, he met her again and 'felt the impulse to put her on the train there and then, and take her away'. But they had hardly spoken to each other when the guard sounded the bell, and he had to hurry back while hating the guard for doing that.

From that time on, the desire to see the girl became an obsession. Each time he passed Deoli, he would direct his gaze station-ward 'half-expecting to see the same unchanged face smiling up at me', but she was nowhere to be found. He felt the overwhelming desire to hunt every nook and corner of Deoli in search of the girl. He asked the station master her whereabouts; but let the matter rest there saying, 'But I will never break my journey there. It may spoil my game'.

In 'A Phone Call', a short story by Dorothy Parker, a girl wallows in self-pity as the call she expects from her boyfriend does not come. When her anxiety becomes unbearable, she starts counting five hundred by fives hoping that the call will come before she completes her counting. The girl knows for sure that she won't get the call, but keeps on hoping. The story ends there, leaving the reader in a state of agony. But Bond ends his story differently. At the end he declares that 'an artist must know where to stop, otherwise his art may suffer'.

In his story, the narrator, despite his hard-to-resist longing to break the journey at Deoli, never does so, for the reason that all the life-sustaining emotion that the girl has given rise to, may suffer a setback.

Bond's commitment to writing is fierce. He is not prepared to trade his passionate passion to paint the details of life's idiosyncrasies for anything. He seems to advise through this story that one has to keep the hope alive until the last moment of one's life. So one should let mystery remain a mystery. When one unravels it, one virtually spoils it.

The effortless and spontaneous manner of his expression, the brevity of the length of his story, his exemplary manner of holding nothing back from the reader, and his extraordinary 'Negative Capability'—all this has helped Bond achieve a rare intimacy with his Indian readers. 'I've always felt that India is my home', Bond confides.

The Liberating Force of Ruskin Bond's Poetry

He does not tell it slant; he tells it straight. He expresses himself just as he feels. And it does not make his poems any less poetic. Rather, this manner of speaking his heart out without experimenting too much with word, form and syntax, has brought him, quite naturally, very close to his Indian readers who feel as if he is one of their own. The only conditions that Ruskin Bond as a poet imposes on his readers are that they must have mountains in their blood; they must have a dream worth pursuing; and they must be stripped of their egos so that they can view the cosmic wonders with the eyes of a child.

Let us first discuss the poem titled 'The Fern'. In this poem, one can find symbols culled only from Mother Nature. The poet says:

The slender maidenhair fern grows firm on a rock
While all around her the water swirls and chatters
And then disappears in a rush
Down to the bottom of the hill.
When I'm surrounded by troubled waters, Lord,
Let me find within a rock to cling to,
And give me the quiet patience of the maidenhair
Who has learned to live with the rock.

The poet here takes heart from the slender maidenhair fern, which is really at the mercy of the stupendous force of Nature just like human beings. But at a time when we tend to crumble and give in, this fern made up of fine stalks and delicate fronds courageously puts its head up while the menacing water threatens to wipe it out of the rock on which it grows, firm and undaunted.

The poet, caught in the whirlpool of life, does not want to meekly submit to the whims and fancies of fate, but instead wants to cultivate a sort of limitless patience so that he could follow in the footsteps of Marcus Aurelius who says that one must be like a promontory of the sea, against which though the waves beat continuously, yet it stands and about it are those swelling waves stilled and quieted. Prof R.P. Chaddah rightly says in an article from the book *The Creative Contours of Ruskin Bond*, edited by Dr Prabhat K. Singh, that this poem 'develops into a symbol of life and creation which is able to withstand the blows of time . . . .'

In 'Kites', the poet compares a kite-maker with a man who composes poems. The poem goes like this:

Are you listening to me, boy?
I'm only your kite-maker,
My poems are flimsy things
Torn by the wind, caught in mango trees,
Gay sport for boys and dreamers.
My silent songs. But once I fashioned
A kite like a violin,
She sang most mournfully, like the wind
In tall Deodars . . .
. . . Boy, are you
Listening? All my kites
Are torn, but for you I'll make a bright
New poem to fly.

A kite, when it's cut loose, lands nobody knows where. No one can say for sure whether it remains whole or gets torn. Similarly, when a poem is published, the poet does not know exactly which corner or stand it is likely to hit. That is to say he cannot know who actually reads it and whether the poem is given its due. The poet laments the fact that the critics generally make mincemeat of it without caring for it at all. A poem, which he calls a 'silent song', is not taken seriously. A poem in his hand reaches the level of soulful music 'like the wind in tall deodars', but sadly goes unnoticed, because to most of us it is a 'flimsy thing'. And yet the poet is determined to continue to craft out poems with invisible wings which like the kite can fly. Bond here brings out poignantly the apathy with which poetry in general is treated.

In 'Rain in the Hills', the poet creates a meditative mood looking at the steady drift of raindrops falling in rhythm with the movement of the soul:

In the hushed silence of the house
When I am quite alone . . .
. . . I sit in a liquid silence, a silence within,
Surrounded by the rhythm of rain
The steady drift
Of water on leaves, on lemons, on roof,
Drumming on drenched dahlias and window panes,
While the mist holds the house in a dark caress.

The poem is like a painting. The words sketch the figure of a persona sitting all alone near the window overlooking a vast expanse of rolling hills (not yet completely denuded). The continuous patterned fall of rain on the trees, the windows spattered with drops of rain giving a somewhat distorted picture of the drenched world outside, and the mist, like a haze of clouds clinging at the outer ring of the full moon, surrounding the house as if caressing it as the darkness slowly gathers around it, complete the picture of a man in a meditative repose.

In 'Hold on to Your Dreams', Bond exhorts all those who have a dream to follow, to go the whole hog, and not abandon the ship in mid-ocean.

> Hold on to your dreams,
> Do not let them die.
> We are lame without them—
> Birds that cannot fly.

Remember *Zorba the Greek*, *Jonathan Livingston Seagull*, or *The Alchemist*? Or, for that matter, *An Artist of the Floating World*? The central thread in each one of these timeless books is the same: Once you discover your passion, your dream, the merest mention of which helps you concentrate within yourself, never look back, but advance, no matter how the outside world treats you. The words of the famous Lebanese-American poet Kahlil Gibran are in the same vein:

'Advance, and never halt, for advancing is perfection. Advance and never fear the thorns in the path, for they draw only corrupt blood.'

You must, as Bond says elsewhere, be able to put your disappointments behind you. And then while undertaking the hard work, if you somehow manage to negotiate successfully with the strange twists and turns in your life, a day will certainly arrive to give you the reasons for pursuing your dream.

So many people give up, overcome by the struggle and doubt; some others never even try to seek the purpose of existence, or to justify it to themselves. A man without a dream is like a bird without a wing. A wingless bird and a lame man are just the same. If pursued in right earnest, your dream can bring about a metamorphosis within you, for there is a magic, says Paulo

Coelho, 'in the excitement of the unexpected, in the desire to do something with real fervour, in the certainty that one is going to realise a dream. Passion sends us signals that guide us throughout our lives'.

In 'Raindrop', Bond brings us face to face with the creator of the cosmos. He makes us realise that the earth where we live, however gigantic the seas and the mountains appear before our eyes, is just like a raindrop in the hand of God. Just try to imagine the profundity and perception of God.

This leaf so complete in itself
Is only part of a tree.
And this tree so complete in itself,
Is only part of the mountain.
And the mountains run down to the sea.
And the sea, so complete in itself,
Rest like a raindrop
In the hand of God.

Right from the tiniest creation to the mind-boggling depth of the sea or sky-kissing height of the mountains, there is a stamp of sheer perfection in everything around us created by the hand of an unseen presence. But the earth is just a tiny dot on the map of the universe, the entire periphery of which still remains unknown. If one looks at the discovered part of the universe, there are trillions of earth-like areas on the map. This solar system, whose magnitude defies human imagination, is governed by the greatest artiste. Bond takes the micro, marvelling all the while at its beauty and completeness, and then slowly moves towards the macro, which is just as complete and perfect.

The poet knows that what lies beyond visual range light years away from the earth, is, unlike earth, infinite and therefore immeasurable. So in the hands of the governor up there, the creator of the universe, the sea with its seemingly boundless expanse 'rests like a raindrop'.

Think of the density of a neutron star which is hundreds of million tons per cubic inch. Unbelievable, isn't it? Nothing, including light, can ever escape from the core of a black hole. Call it an act of god or force of gravity, whatever you wish.

The inner message here is – The ego of human beings is absolutely misplaced. No human being, or all of us put together, can ever approach, let alone equal, the majesty of God. Therefore, realising this, a man should always remain humble; whatever might be the nature of his accomplishment.

Let us now turn to another poem of Bond – 'Hill Station':

There is nothing to keep me here,
Only these mountains of silence
And the gentle reserve of shepherds and woodmen
Who know me as one who
Walks among trees.

Madman, misanthropist? They make
Their guesses, smile and pass slowly
Down the steep path near the cottage.
There is nothing
To keep me here, walking
Among old trees.

In 'Lost all my Money', Bond writes: 'Nothing in the city but a sickness of the soul'. Those of us who live in the city and have visited Landour, where Bond resides, are likely to realise that the city people, most of them, would do well to go for an attitude overhaul. The poet is only interested in digging into the treasure trove lying within rather than without. And the madding crowds in the city, who accord top priority to making money, actually destroy good souls.

In 'The father, the Son' (from *The Way Things Are*), Roger McGough writes:

> It is unusual to find me here, in town.
> I never did like crowds. The smell,
> The dust, the racket. I can do without it . . .
> Too many leeches with too much to lose
> The mobsters, the spies, the black marketers.
> Too many fingers in too many pies.
> The backhanders, the sweeteners . . .
> The wheeler-dealers, the sultans of sleaze.
> The ones who feed on the carrion of conflict
> Who profit from the status quo
> Who fuel the hatreds that keep
> The tribes apart. Who know
> That where there's fear, there's money.

Bond feels exactly the way poet Roger McGough does. An artiste dissolved in the divine task of unravelling the mystery of life has no interest whatsoever to waste the precious time in amassing wealth or get preoccupied with worthless earth-bound pursuits that stand in the way of 'finding the centre'. But there is a price to be paid for taking the road that yields nothing for you in monetary terms.

People who are blissfully oblivious of cultivating their own gardens call the poet mad and a misanthrope. But the poet does not mind them any more. He carries on with his self-imposed task, regardless.

The poem 'Walk Tall' is very inspiring in that it imparts the age-old wisdom: 'know thyself'.

You stride through the long grass,
Pressing on over fallen pine-needles,
Up the winding road to the mountain-pass:
Small red ant, now crossing a sea
Of rain drops; your destiny
To carry home that single, slender cosmos seed,
Waving it like a banner in the sun.

Have you ever seen an army of red ants marching up or down a crevice or a wall, each carrying crumbs heavier than its body weight? Their purpose is single-minded, total commitment, labouring up all the way to its destination. If you observe nature to the exclusion of everything else, a time may come when you will be able to read the script of nature's language, its signs and wonders.

The poet, a compulsive walker, chugs up the winding mountain road all alone one day when 'small red ants . . . crossing a sea of raindrops' catch his attention. Watching them, it suddenly dawns on him that everyone of us here on earth has a specific purpose in life. Once the purpose comes to light, it is everyone's duty, like the ant, to fulfill that purpose. It may be something as simple as carrying home the materials needed for survival. Or it may be learning the language of nature in order to strive to explore one's roots.

Whatever it might be, one must have the courage of one's conviction to stick it out through to the end 'waving it like a banner in the sun'. What others do, whether they fare better in life than you do is not your concern. Once you discover the purpose of your existence, a purpose you instinctively know to be uniquely made for you alone; look nowhere else, walk tall, be proud of yourself, sure in the belief that you are capable of dealing with anything.

Bond writes in lapidary style. Like the English version of *Gitanjali* that fetched Rabindranath Tagore the Nobel Prize in

Literature, Bond's poems are highly transparent, almost like the crystal clear water of a brook through which you can see the riverbed without any semblance of scum blocking the view or hiding parts of it. His poems yield themselves to anyone who has an eye for nature's wonders. Above all, his poems are able to release the pent-up feelings in the reader's mind. It has that unique power capable of liberating any soul caught in the throes of modern-day sickness born out of the penchant to run after money and fame.

Ruskin Bond in Conversation

A Strange Kinship

On a sudden impulse, I reached Mussoorie the other day, saturated with just one longing too intense – to see Ruskin Bond. As the twilight was deepening into darkness outside, I, with my heart going thump-thump, dialled his number from inside the Padmini Niwas reception room.

'Could I speak to Mr Ruskin Bond please?'

'Speaking!'

'Sir, I'm . . . I've come all the way from Calcutta (now Kolkata) just to see you. Could I?'

'Where are you?'

'At hotel Padmini Niwas, near Library Stand.'

'How long you're going to stay up here?'

'Till twenty-fourth instant, Sir.'

'You can come tomorrow at four in the afternoon. In between four and half past four. Okay? You know the way to my cottage?'

I must have sounded a little uncertain when I said 'yes'. He mapped out the path that leads to his residence, adding: 'Ask anybody at Landour. You'll be shown the way'. When he expressed the hope to see me the next day, I wished him 'Goodnight' and hung up feeling a strange kinship with him.

Mr Bond received me as I climbed a few steps leading to the entrance of his cottage. To me it was more a dream than reality—a stranger from Calcutta in the company of a first-rate writer. But since I have been soaking up his stories for the last so many years, I did not feel particularly shy talking to him about himself.

Author: *When did he make his first attempt at writing?*

Ruskin Bond: 'When I was probably in class seventh or eighth, I did attempt a little novel about school life. It did not survive. Since it had some remarks directed against my teachers, some other boy or teacher got hold of it, and you know . . . But it was nothing special. It was an early attempt.'

A: *For Jack London it was Quida's* Signa *that turned him to writing. For Bond, did the initial inspiration lay in some other source?*

RB: 'I must have been about thirteen to fourteen years old when I read *David Copperfield* (by Charles Dickens) and *Fortitude* (by Hugh Walpole) and I wanted to be a writer.'

A: *Does his entry into the world of creative writing have something in common with writers like Leo Tolstoy, Guy de Maupassant, Virginia Woolf, Rudyard Kipling and others, in the sense that all of them could rise to prominence because of their habit of diary-writing?*

RB: 'My first novel grew out of diary-writing. The first draft was in diary or journal form. The publisher suggested that I turn it into a novel. As I did so, it became somewhat fictionalised. I changed it from first to third person and brought in other characters and incidents. So finally, after two or three drafts, they accepted it.'

A: *In the first novel* The Room on the Roof, *one finds that the characters are all Indian.*

RB: 'In fact, it was written out of a sort of homesickness for the friends I had grown up with in India.'

A: *Did he ever follow, while learning the craft, the usages of other great authors?*

RB: 'I guess I wanted to emulate my favourite authors, you know. That was part of it.'

A: *What about the prospects of being a writer in those days?*

RB: 'In those days there were very few magazines, papers and publishers; almost non-existent as far as literature went. I mean there were lots of textbook publishers, but very few published in the way of a novel.'

A: *Tragedy crept over his childhood when his mother decided to move out with someone else. To make matters tragically worse, the only ballast-lending being on earth, his dearest father was wrenched away from him by the cruel hands of fate when he was only ten. It was a great blow, for no other person could fill the immense void created by his father's untimely death. What about his stepfather?*

RB: 'Looking back on it, my stepfather was never unkind; just rather indifferent. Perhaps, he did not have an understanding of children. He did not have time for children too. He was just like that. He did not mean any harm.'

A: *And his mother?*

RB: 'She had her own individuality. She was very attractive. She did not have the literary bent. Although we did quarrel, we generally got on very well. As I grew older, I think I came to a better understanding. Normally when you're very small, you become resentful.'

While talking of trees and flowers, Bond suddenly remembered Bishal Ohri, the manager at the State Bank of India (SBI), Mussoorie.

RB: 'He is a good friend of mine, you know. He is a nature lover, always looking for wild flowers. He is in one of my books. I wrote about him.'

When I expressed the overpowering desire to see the room where he etched his cameos, he accompanied me to his study-cum-bedroom, and opened the window that overlooks a breath-taking view of the heaving mountain ranges, hemmed in with blue-green mist. A whiff of chilly wind blew in.

He brought my notice to the forty-year-old typewriter, his only asset other than his books, more precious than a word-processor or anything that the world could buy.

One hour galloped by as if in the blink of an eye. But it was enough to cement the bond between the wonder-eyed, romance-smitten, unforgettable character Rusty, and me.

Once out of his house, I kept stopping in my tracks, looking at his modest cottage which houses his invisible muse as if in a trance.

So many other people tread the road beneath his window, which winds its way to mysterious places. The pristine poplar, the opulent oak, the fantastic fir, they all line the road for everyone to take sustenance from. But it is to Ruskin Bond, among a selected few, that they talk and confide their tales of woe. They give company to him when harsh reality grates on his nerves, so that his genius, undistracted by the hype and hoopla all around, continues to produce spirit-lifting work of immortal nature as before.

When I returned to Padmini Niwas where I was staying, it was not dark yet. Standing on the balcony, I started reading Bond's last entry in his book, *Rain in the Mountains*, which Mr Bond had gifted to me. Imbued with a rare sense of fulfilment, I was dipping in his soul-stuff, amazed at his ability to take the reader along with him. However, only those readers endowed with a special spiritual streak, a sense of compassion, and a commitment that has nothing to do with any material advancement, can catch the waves his pen emits.

(First published in *Garhwal Post*)

Friendly with a Crow

Fatherless, when not yet an adolescent, forsaken by his own mother, ill-treated by some of his relatives, the rare realisation that the release from cramp and confinement of existence could be made possible through writing dawned on Ruskin Bond when he was just a schoolboy. He never looked back, and made history when only seventeen years old, by winning an international award for his *The Room on the Roof.* He had stints as a junior clerk in a solicitor's office, as an assistant in a travel agency, and as the editor of *Imprint.* But ultimately, he has chosen the freedom to live in a poverty of his own choice, the freedom of the writer.

The spirit of the poplar, of the horizon wrapped in myth and legend, of the simple man who chug-chugs along the steep path of life – all these factors permeate his writing. The heaving mountains, the purl of a runnel, the crease of a stone, and the tinct of spring in the Garhwal's apparelling never escape his inner eye. When we read his stories and poems, we realise that which Wordsworth had said: 'Nature never did betray the heart that loved her'.

Ruskin Bond, whose only ambition was to be a writer, could well have been a legendary teacher, for he is as rare a speaker as a writer. One only has to listen to his articulation, intonation and accentuation to be convinced of his superb dialogue-writing skills, which reminds one of Hemingway and Fitzgerald, especially.

Just as Emily Bronte's Gondal, James Joyce's Dublin and Gustave Flaubert's Rouen live on, so will Ruskin Bond's Dehra and Mussoorie. Bond captures the myriad moods of sleepy hill towns of India with a finesse that tends to follow the Iceberg Theory of Ernest Hemingway. Bond, like Hemingway, seems to believe that art lies in concealing art. And as a result, readers do not have to toil upward in the night to read him.

Reading a Bond story is like watching a glorious sunset. The story, like the sunset, fades out. But what is experienced is preserved in the store of the reader's memory forever.

Bond spins his stories with a stunning frankness. His uncommonly common, biblical, clear-window style of writing has become a model for so many young writers since. No anthology of world's best contemporary stories will be complete without his contribution.

A: *'The introductions to the collections of your stories, novels, and poems, read like stories themselves. Have you ever thought of publishing all the introductions together in a single volume?'*

RB: 'Well, that's an interesting idea. In fact, when Penguin were preparing that omnibus volume—*Collected Stories and Novels*, and another anthology called *Best of Ruskin Bond*—I had, in fact, suggested that some of my introductions be included. But they didn't take me seriously. A lot of introductions to different collections or books tell you something about myself or about how I came to write the stories. Since most of them were done for the Penguin collections, I'd have to persuade them to agree to such a proposal . . . Maybe you could write and suggest it!'

A: *'Some time back, you gave readings from your writings meant for children in the capital, arranged by the British Council library in New Delhi. A drama was also staged based on your works. How did it go?'*

RB: 'I had quite an enjoyable experience. It was the first time virtually that I'd given such readings because it's not normally a popular thing in India. I mean you get poetry recitation in Urdu, Hindi, and other languages, but authors actually reading from their books is not very common. There were both young and old people in the audience who seemed to enjoy it.

'I read a couple of essays and macabre tales like "A Face in the Dark". Then I read a couple of light pieces – one about my walking habits and another about the night the roof blew off, the very roof you're sitting beneath, and then a couple of poems.'

A: *'Were there any questions from the audience?'*

RB: 'They asked me questions for more than half an hour. It was like an interview. One boy asked me if I believe in ghosts. I said, "No, but I keep seeing them!" Another voice said, "We want more action in your stories, Mr Bond." I said, "All right, I'll try!" Though I'm not really much of an action writer.

'Then one little boy made a very intelligent question. He asked, "Why is there no children's newspaper?" And everybody laughed. That's a very good idea. I mean we get children supplements in newspapers. But there's no actual children's newspaper which is largely written by them. Of course, it'd mean somebody perhaps promoting it or financing it to begin with. It could even catch on.'

A: *'Was the poem "Lost" your very first write-up published in* The Illustrated Weekly *way back in 1952?'*

RB: 'It was certainly the first published poem. But there were at least one or two stories published before. One of them was 'My Calling'. It was a sketch about one of my schoolteachers. I wrote it just after leaving school. I've never included it in a book or collection, nor have I reprinted it. I thought it was a little work of a novice. It was my first attempt, you know.'

A: *'Your tremendous love for your father creeps out in almost every piece that you write. You seem to be still smarting from your father's untimely death. Have you, through writing, exorcised the ghost of this extremely painful memory?'*

RB: 'I guess I have. You see, in my day-to-day contemporary life there's no one alive today who'd have known my father, at least nobody I'm in touch with. So it's not possible to talk about him to anyone who knew him.

'He was not a very sociable man, you know. So may be in writing about him, I'm at least having a dialogue with my medium about him, and it also helps me to express the debt I feel to him—that he perhaps gave me the love for books, of quite a side of life. But I think having lost one's father when one is so young, one is inclined to put him on a pedestal.

'He may not have been the perfect father or a perfect individual; but childhood impressions, you know, are inclined to make him appear that way.'

A: *'You had an arrest warrant issued against you for writing an allegedly obscene novella,* The Sensualist.'

RB: 'The Sensualist was first serialised in *Debonair*, Bombay, during 1974-75. Someone there, I'm not quite sure who, may be an official, had taken an objection to it; got someone to complain; and obscenity charges were brought against me, the editor, and the publisher of the magazine. As a result of which, an arrest warrant came to Mussoorie. I got the bail, of course. Formally, I was arrested; briefly. Though long enough to have tea and biscuits with the officials! I had to attend the court twice.'

A: *'Did it affect you in any way?'*

RB: 'At the start it did; I was a bit worried. Having a pessimistic mind and being the worrying kind, I thought of worst possibilities such as spending seven years in Bombay Central Jail or something of that nature! I guess these things happen from time to time. Many writers have similar experiences.'

A: *'You have dedicated some of your poems and stories to one elusive Binya. Is she known to you?'*

RB: 'Well, she was a part dream, part real girl who used to live on the hillside decades ago. I was in Maplewood Lodge then. When I often want to write a story around a girl character, she sort of comes to mind. You need a role model, don't you? As a child she is in "Blue Umbrella", a little older in "Binya Passes By". There are also a couple of love poems on her.'

A: *'In* Thus Spoke Crow *you've laid down certain rules for all artistes, that is, not to want too much too soon, not to fret, etc. Will you please elaborate on that?'*

RB: 'In that piece, wasn't I sharing a bottle of beer with a crow? So may be under the influence of it I might have propounded certain philosophies which may not be too practical!

'I think that the time when I wrote it, I had been strongly influenced by Taoism, by Lao Tzu, the ancient Chinese philosopher. I think I had been reading his works, and some of the advice that I gave, or the crow gave to me, was partly Taoist. It applied to my situation as a struggling writer too. The piece of advice I then gave myself was – don't pursue things, let them pursue you.'

A: *'In the first part of your memoir you have taken into consideration the time upto the age of twenty-one, haven't you?'*

RB: 'Yes. Looking back, it seems more eventful in those first twenty-one years. I suppose it's for most people. The last twenty or thirty years have been, more or less, placid, writing steadily, you know. From the work point of view, I've done more in the last few years. But growing up years were more interesting; the people you knew then, those early struggles. So the first part would be more interesting for me, possibly for the reader too, and the later years for a writer.'

A: '*In which way is the second part of your autobiography*—The Lamp is Lit—*different from* Scenes from a Writer's Life?'

RB: 'It's not written in that sort of chapter-by-chapter method I used in *Scenes from a Writer's Life*. It's more a collection of essays, which look back on my life as a freelance—zigzagging along from the age of twenty-one to the present.'

A: '*Have you ever pardoned Mr Priestley, the headmaster who promised to give your father's letters back to you, but didn't?*'

RB: 'Of course, yes. In the story I've dramatised it a bit; I don't think it was deliberate. But I felt very resentful at that time. How could he be so absent-minded or careless. He was probably overworked!'

A: '*You said elsewhere that your life once depended upon your story-telling abilities in many ways. Is that why you never wholly caught up with human relationships?*'

RB: 'I think what I meant there was that storytelling is one of the few things I do well. So I had to earn a living by telling stories. I'd be hopeless working in a bank, or teaching in a school. In being a writer, you've got to interact with people; It is very important. But I'm not really alone. I live with Prem and his family, which has grown with time. When I want to be alone, I take a walk. A lot of people ask me why I never married. I think it's just something that might have happened but did not.'

A: '*The producer of the film* Junoon, *based on your novella* A Flight of Pigeons *didn't do justice to you, financially. Your comments, please.*'

RB: 'The film *Junoon* (not to be confused with the TV serial by the same name) was made by Shyam Benegal in 1980. Yes, I didn't get very much. But then having once accepted it, I had no other way but to shrug it off. It's alright though; I think I am to blame!'

A: *'Was the film successful from the financial and the artistic point of view?'*

RB: 'I believe it did quite well. Financially, it was successful for the producer. Good acting and characterisation, in the first half, particularly.

'There's no significant change from the original story until the end. They gave it a rather dramatic ending. In the original, the Pathan family is very much a middle class, or lower middle class family, living in the back streets. In the film it was given an opulent look . . . I think there may have been . . . a slight influence from *Shatranj Ke Khiladi,* which was made a couple of years before my *A Flight of Pigeons* was made into a film.'

A: *'In* The Adventures of Rusty, *you wrote: ". . . ports had . . . the most romantic association for me. . . ." Have you ever written anything on sea-matters barring your "Escape from Java".'*

RB: 'Had I spent more time by the sea, I'd have probably written more about it. But apart from my childhood in Jamnagar, and a couple of years that I spent in the Channel Islands in Jersey, my experience at sea is little. Living by the sea is not the same as actually being at sea or making a life as a seafarer, which would have given me the subject matter. It's something that in another life I'd have done.'

A: *'You've received the Sahitya Akademi Award, John L. Rhys Award, British Award for Commonwealth Writer, Padmoshri from the Government of India, and N.D. Mehra Memorial Award. You have also been nominated twice for Hans Christian Anderson Award . . . Does fame interfere with your daily schedule of writing?'*

RB: 'Sometimes I wish I was the unknown writer of thirty years ago, when I could compose my stories and vignettes without interruption!'

A: *'You always write out of your own personal experience, don't you?'*

RB: 'Very much out of my own life, yes. Not always though. There are stories (like 'A Flight of Pigeons') which were not written exactly out of my own experience, but which had something of typical experience to me.

'But then I'm a subjective writer, and I suppose you get the other kind of writers who are usually more successful . . . Bestselling writers of today tell a story in which they are not involved in any way, you know. And if it's something sensational, it makes more money. . . .'

A: *'Do you still write your diary?'*

RB: 'In recent years, my diary has more been a record of funny things that have happened to me. I think, as we grow older, we should not take ourselves too seriously. So it's more in the form of a humourist diary rather than *The Diary of a Nobody* by Grossmith . . . But when I was younger, I took myself more seriously and put down thoughts that I thought were great, but later turned out to be not so great!'

A: *'I believe quite a few scholars are now working on your stories and novels. Are they in touch with you?'*

RB: 'Quite a few are getting in touch or making enquiries. Debasish Banerjee from Calcutta is doing some research on my work. Amita Aggrawal from Saharanpur is doing her doctorate on "The Fictional World of Ruskin Bond". Then there's a couple in Bombay, someone in Indore, Achal Sinha from St. Xavier's college, Ranchi . . . I don't remember all the names. I can't correspond as much as I like to, but I try.

'There's a lady, you know, who came to see me the other day; met me for the first time. She'd recently discovered my stories. She was very keen to see the house of my grandmother, which I wrote about in some stories of my childhood years at Dehradun. I told her where it is, but I also warned her that it has changed a lot too . . . because it has some structural changes though the basic house is still there. So I told her: "Go and have a look at it". But I've not had a report from her yet!'

A: *'There are other memorable descriptions also in your stories of places like the maidan. . . .'*

RB: 'The maidan is still there but full of potholes having all sorts of circuses and exhibitions all round the year.'

A: *'The room on the roof?'*

RB: 'It's got swallowed up! The building on which it used to perch is still there, but the building has got converted into a four or five storey structure. So the room is somewhere swallowed up in the first or the second floor. You can't see it any more though it probably exists in some form. That old building has now become a school.'

A: *'And the bazaars in Dehradun?'*

RB: 'They're very much the same, the Paltan bazaar and the Dhamowala bazaar. Now it's a little more crowded. Traffic can't really go through except for bicycles and scooters. They remain much as they used to be.'

A: *'You used to write in the proximity to nature, under a tree for example. Do you still do that?'*

RB: 'I think it's the one I described in *Cherry Tree & Other Stories*. That's near the place where I lived previously – Maplewood Lodge. I often wrote beneath that tree. Here (Ivy Cottage where Mr Bond lives now), the room is quite sunny. A little way up from here, there are some lovely spots where one can sit down and write.

'Strangely enough, I work harder now in my advancing years than when I was younger because I am better organised at home . . . my letters, manuscripts, papers, etc. I sort of got used to working at the desk. If I go for a walk, I might carry a notebook and make the odd note.

'But I'd not perhaps sit down under a tree now to write a complete story. I'd find it easier at my desk. Although there was a time when I used to do that. There were one or two stories like "Love is a Sad Song" which I actually wrote out on the hillside under the cherry tree. It'd still be there . . . But I can write anywhere if the mood is upon me—in the train, in a crowded house. . . .'

A: *'Late J. Ramadurai recounted in one of the articles that he once found you typing in a bus. Do you remember that?'*

RB: 'I can't remember that! There's this gentleman who I met years back in Delhi when I was freelancing. Apparently I inspired him to take up journalism . . . He said he found me typing in a bus. But you can't type in a Delhi or Calcutta bus. You go mad! It'd be too jerky, people getting in and out. May be you could scribble a note. I don't know whether he made it up! But he probably encountered me when I was bringing my typewriter home after giving it somewhere for repairs. Maybe the bus was stationary, and I might have opened it up and put in a paper. At that point of time I did have a column, *Random Reflections*, which I used to do for *Hindustan Times*, some forty years back.'

A: *'Some of your stories remind one of H.E. Bates. Did you ever read his stories?'*

RB: 'I started reading Bates when I was at school . . . basically his short stories which always charmed me, and he writes very sensitively of nature and the countryside which had an influence on me in some way.'

A: *'William Golding?'*

RB: 'Haven't read much of his. But I had read his *Lord of the Flies* years back.'

A: *'And what about F. Scott Fitzgerald?'*

RB: 'He's a favourite of mine. Only the other day I was re-reading *The Great Gatsby*. I have read that about three times, you know. I often go back to some writers. I've also been reading (Virginia) Woolf more in recent years than I did when I was younger. I can appreciate her better now.'

A: *'Who, according to you, is an ideal interviewer?'*

RB: 'Someone like you! Someone who asks questions relating to one's work and writing and reading . . . I don't give many interviews—perhaps four or five in a year at the most. You take the trouble to come up here (Landour, Mussoorie) and meet me. Otherwise, sometimes when I'm in Delhi for a few days, people attached to newspapers or magazines come to know one's in town, and interview one. Perhaps they don't see me in my natural home or set-up. Questions are often limited to what I'm actually doing in Delhi or what my latest book in the making is . . . natural enough.'

A: *'Now that your place is secure in the world of writing, do you sometimes look back and marvel at the manner in which you've gone from strength to strength?'*

RB: 'Over the decades I've always gone from strength to strength in a way . . . I'm not like a forgotten writer of the fifties or sixties. More people read me today, and I write more today than I did then . . . I'm fortunate that there're young readers who're discovering or reading for the first time what I might have written twenty or thirty years back. All the works that I did over the years have not gone down the river.'

A: *'You've recreated your childhood days at Jamnagar with a rare artistry. The palace you grew up in has become a place of tourist interest. What do you have to say?'*

RB: 'Well, I'd hesitate to go to Jamnagar to take a look at those palaces now as it would destroy the picture I have in mind. Now it's almost a fairy tale memory of being a small child and seeing what were lovely palaces in those days. By now, I believe, they must have become government houses or would have been converted into other sorts of buildings, and would have inevitably lost their charm and beauty. The palaces, I think, are now utilised for different purposes. Still, it's nice to know there are people who like to see the places I write about.'

A: *'In one of your stories you mention that you compose first in your head down to the last word before committing it to paper. How do you do that?'*

RB: 'Not exactly down to the last word but a fairly clear idea of what I'm going to put down and how. What inspires me? I don't know myself. Sometimes I get an idea or inspiration from something I might observe on a walk or from my window or anywhere. And then I put it in words. At other times I might just sit down at my desk with a totally blank mind and as soon as I've got a pen in my hand, things start flowing. The ideas or thoughts come to me simply from the process of virtually sitting down to write, there's no hard and fast rule.

'For example, yesterday I sat down to write a story. But then suddenly changed my mind and wrote on a totally different subject. It was a story but it was not the one I sat down to write! So sometimes, you know, there's no particular planning involved. But usually, once I've started a story or an essay, I go through with it. It's not often that I abandon it halfway through. That happens, but very rarely. So once I've written a page or two, I carry on and finish it, to whatever length it happens to be.'

A: *'How did you develop such extraordinary dialogue-writing skills? Did you ever think of being a playwright?'*

RB: 'You see, I used to read a lot of Shaw, O'Neill, Tennessee Williams as well as playwrights like (Somerset) Maugham. Perhaps I would have even written plays but for the fact that it commands a very small market here. To be a playwright, ideally you should be settled in London or New York. Having permanently settled in India, I never really pursued that line.'

A: *'In your memoir you wrote: "We don't become writers in schools of creative writing. We become writers before we learn to write." What exactly did you mean?'*

RB: 'I think I meant that learning the craft itself is not going to make you a writer, unless the urge is already there in you. Schools of writing can be useful, but if it's not part of your make-up, it's not going to turn you into anything more than maybe just a competent writer.'

A: *'How did you develop love for your medium of expression?'*

RB: 'I guess it's because one grows up living in literature and books and the more one reads, the more one learns to appreciate the styles and nuances of various writers . . . You could get hundreds of writers using English as a medium of expression and yet each one would be different if they were good writers. That's where, you see, my criticism of the schools of creative writing comes in because writers who have gone through these schools, often come out writing the same way. If you come across the works of some writers who have been through these creative schools, there's always the similarity of style, of the use of language . . . I also think that the English language lends itself to individuality of expression.'

A: *'Not many are aware that the Boston University, where your manuscripts are now well preserved, has accorded you a rare honour. When and how did you receive the prestigious offer from the University?'*

RB: 'About a decade ago, they wrote to me out of the blue. I received a letter from the director of Boston University, Dr Gotlieb. They have a special collection library of twentieth century authors where they have a section on Indian writers. I think there are several other Indian writers who are also represented there.'

A: *'Could you please recall what you said in your Sahitya Akademi address?'*

RB: 'I took my award and ran! I do my best to avoid getting up on a rostrum even if it's only to avoid saying a few words! By the way, I gave a talk recently; just an informal talk. It's called Rosalind Wilson Memorial Lecture. It went off quite well. I reminisced about my love of books and how I became a writer myself.'

A: *'In* A Handful of Nuts *one gets the picture of a writer who feels the need to confide in someone. It seemed that terrible loneliness stalked you throughout your life. Does the past still trouble you at times?'*

RB: 'I think writers, like most people, need to confide in someone. Because I've lived in places like Mussoorie and Dehradun, where writers are few and far between, there has always been a void within me.

'Maybe it is also an advantage, as it has kept me natural in my writing. As for the past, it does not trouble me. I am pretty much at peace with my present situation and myself. At the same time, I know I've not lived up to my full potential . . . By nature, I am a compulsive writer. There never was any question of that state of retiring. Even when I am not writing a book or a novel, I keep a journal or a diary.'

A: *'You've been freelancing for almost five decades now. How difficult was it to sustain yourself through freelancing initially?'*

RB: 'You see, I was so committed to being a writer that I was prepared for all kinds of struggles. I think one has to be totally committed to writing and not to the idea of fame or money, which may be elusive. But if it does not come, many people give up.

'In my case, fame and riches did not come but I was determined to continue. I was not much good at anything else, you see. So I think I at least chose something that I knew I could do fairly well and stuck to it. So, I've no regrets at all. I have been very fortunate, though it has been a slow process.'

Fictional World of Ruskin Bond

I was speaking to Padmashri Ruskin Bond from Prof Ganesh Saili's (another prominent author associated with Mussoorie and Landour) residence, which is just one hairpin bend below Bond's Ivy cottage. The interview with the English professor was about to be over. I was to leave Mussoorie the very next day. I had already met Bond a couple of days back. I asked him over the professor's cordless telephone whether he would allow me to see him the second time around?

'Oh yes!' the writer told me. He said he would be happy to have me by his side as he was expecting a scholar from Saharanpur that very evening.

Gentle readers of Bond, if you've not met him in person as yet, try speaking to him over the phone any time between 4.00 pm and 4.30 pm. At that time, he is usually home, getting ready for a trudge along the now-sloping-down-now-sloping-up road sculpted out of the Garhwal mountain ranges. He speaks, as he writes, only that which his heart prompts him to. If you're fortunate enough to be in tune with his spirit, a baritone, perfectly accented voice—as pure as a mountain spring—rising or falling according to the divine sentiments lubdubbing within him, will greet you, and you cannot but feel pushed down into the part of your within, where you've never been.

Twilight was about to blur into evening. As I knocked on the door, I noticed a small slip of paper bearing the name of the writer written in long hand stuck on the door. Such fame worldwide and yet the writer lives a simple, unadorned life. A true writer, I realised, does not seek fame or anything associated with it, but only the freedom to express himself.

As Bond ushered me in and we got seated in his drawing room-cum-library, the phone bleeped. Bond scholar Amita had lost her way. The writer, despite a nagging toothache, did not cancel the appointment; he gave her the direction to the Ivy cottage once again. On my request, he inscribed two books of his – *Children's Omnibus* and *A Biography of Nehru*. Then he fell silent.

Within minutes, the scholar arrived with her husband and two lovely children. The introductions over, Amita, working on her thesis entitled 'The Fictional World of Ruskin Bond', set the ball rolling with a question on the woman characters in his stories – whether those remarkably fleshed out characters were real.

'Characters that I fashion out,' said Bond, 'are real sometimes. Not always. Often, the characters are not from real life, not based on anything that happened to me. A lot of people think they're factual but I write in an autobiographical way and put myself in the story. May be that's why people think they're real. Rani (in "The Room of Many Colours") was fictional; real was the palace. Dukhi was based on my grandmother's gardener, which is from a different place and time; and that Rani could have been one of the several Ranis I met! Sushila (in "Love is a Sad Song") is true to some extent. That's based on a diary I kept. That's why it's true. "Time stops at Shamli", one of my first stories, was based on a real character.'

Bond's 'The Woman on Platform 8' was the very first story I read. Both of us were dying to know about the mysterious lady character in the story.

'Here,' said he, 'it is one soul recognising a fellow soul . . . mutual sympathy flowing from one to the other . . . it can be an attraction or an instinctive feeling that the other person is important to you in some way . . . They remind you of something sometimes . . . it's probably one of my own favourites amongst my stories.'

Amita expressed her wonder as to why his stories were mostly based on his childhood.

'From time to time,' mused Bond, 'I feel inclined to go back to it in my writing. Yes, it's a period I can write about quite vividly. I recall and recapture quite well. I recreate that atmosphere quite effectively. But given the choice, I'd rather be living now than in 1945.'

It was my turn. So I asked, 'You are still in love with railway platforms, aren't you?'

'Yes! I like railway platforms. I don't travel much these days . . . But, even now, sometimes, I go down to Dehradun just to sit on the platform for half-an-hour or so and just absorb the atmosphere.'

'Was *The Room on the Roof* symbolic?' Amita's critical faculties were in full cry.

'No, I don't think so. Rain is so important in India, so much a part of everyone's life. May be that's why it comes into my stories so much. Monsoon brings the people to a new life. It also creates a mood, I think.'

Amita then went on to ask why he settled in India of all places?

'I was born here, grew up here . . . Your heart is always where you grew up and where you have your childhood friends. Perhaps I've been reincarnated here two three times as well, even though the last time might have been in a British family . . . In earlier times, may be I was Dukhi, the gardener!'

The Bond scholar was in no mood to give me another chance and went on to ask as to how he would describe friendship.

'I'd say two people who know each other so well that they don't have to talk to each other sometimes. Well, even a marriage—a long lasting one—can be friendship. It's a meeting of two minds on the same wavelength . . . Friendship was an escape for me from an unhappy home life.'

Amita grew a bit bolder. With a tinge of sympathy in her voice, she wanted to know as to why he did not get married.

'I don't know. May be my own disinclination. Romance, but not marriage! One doesn't want to get tied down.'

But why had he not written a single story in which two people did get married?

'All right', Bond chuckled in good humour, 'I'll write a story where two people do get married . . . Now that I'm safe from marriage, I can write one!'

Then both of us gently pestered him to talk about his apprenticeship period. Bond was so involved in the discussion by then that he forgot about his toothache. Fortunately for both of us, he gave an elaborate talk on the writers, teachers and editors who had shown him the gateway to the realm of expression.

'Got influenced by other writers to some extent. I read a lot of essayists like Stevenson, Lamb, Priestley . . . In my teens, I read a lot of Tagore . . . and yes, R.K. Narayan and Mulk Raj Anand, back in fifties and sixties. I was a great reader, a prolific reader, you know.

'And then there were one or two good teachers who took an interest in me and advised me. Mr Whit-Marsh Knight taught me English; he was also a great fan of Dickens like me. He had the collected works of Dickens and he used to let me borrow one at a time.

'Mr Jones used to say: Never use a difficult word if a simple word will express what you want to say better. To him, clarity of expression was more important than getting carried away with verbosity. He was a good teacher.

'There was not much practical help from other writers otherwise. Certainly, there were some editors who encouraged me when I was younger. There was C.R. Mandy of *The Illustrated Weekly*, which was then the premier magazine. He used to publish my earlier stories, back in fifties. *Sunday Statesman* from Calcutta and Delhi published my work. Then there was the *Hindustan Standard* from Calcutta. . . .'

During the interview, Bond received a couple of calls from his artist friends at Landour in Mussoorie. It was obvious that they were feeling Bond's absence. We desperately wanted to be with him for some more time. But an hour-and-a-half had just vanished. Amita requested for one of his photographs with his autograph. Bond obliged her, saying that his photo-bank had a much-depleted stock now.

It was a full moon night. On the way back, our favourite writer accompanied us till the point where he was expected to pass a few moments with his friends. Down below one could see the Doon Valley, studded with beads of diamonds beckoning as if it were a land of dreams. As we parted, he wished us a good trip back. He waited till we disappeared round the bend, just as the protagonists did in so many unforgettable stories of Bond who, according to David Davidar, publisher of Penguin India, 'is certainly one of the big guns in the writer's pantheon' (*Books Today*, April-June 2000).

Getting Through Life Without Too Many Bruises

Strange is the art of reviewing in India. The works of the outstanding writer Ruskin Bond—'resident Wordsworth in prose'—one of the most popular writers in India for decades now, and whose name is synonymous with Landour, Mussoorie, are still at times ruthlessly reviewed.

The very first novel by Bond (*The Room on the Roof*), published for the first time in 1956, is still in print—a great achievement in itself as anyone who is a little conversant with the highly commercialised publishing world is aware how difficult it is to have a book reprinted by publishers of repute at frequent intervals, unless there is a great demand for the same by the readers. Here comes the question, who is more important – the reader or the reviewer? Needless to say, for every writer it is the reader that counts. There are quite a few other books by Bond which have been reprinted more than fifteen times.

In *Landour Days* (published in 2002), Bond writes without mentioning the name of the critic: 'Having just read a nasty review of my last book in *India Today*, I take heart by recalling Hemingway's direct action against [the] critic . . . trouble is, my critic is a woman. I'd lose the wrestling match.' Bond, however, holds no grudge against any critic.

A: *'In your book* Landour Days, *you wrote about the scathing review published in* India Today. *Reading it must have been painful. . . .'*

RB: 'Did I mention it in *Landour Days*? I see, yes. Well, I'd done that piece on famous writers and their critics much earlier. But when I mentioned this particular review which was quite scathing as you say, I joined the two and turned it into an article by using that earlier piece.'

A: *'It must have hurt you. . . .'*

RB: 'One has to get used to these things, you know. I recover very quickly from most things. So probably it had me maybe a little hurt or upset for a few hours. A day or two later, I would have forgotten it or joked about it. One has to expect some amount of criticism. Not everybody is going to like your writing. So, fair enough. I have no complaint or grudge about it. By and large, I've been fairly fortunate in the kind of reviews I've had over the years. Although no review, good or bad, has made any particular difference to the success or otherwise of any of my books.

'Looking back, sometimes books which have got very good reviews have not moved at all; and others which were completely ignored have done quite well. For example, the *Ruskin Bond's Children's Omnibus* published by Rupa & Co. did not need to be sent out to reviewers. It just went into the market and bookshops, and it's in its fifteenth impression after less than ten years . . . Readers will find what they want and what they like.'

A: *'You're also publishing a series of particularly those stories in which Rusty happens to be your alter ego. It's a new kind of thought. . . .'*

RB: 'Quite right. Many of the stories are old stories though. This was actually a concept of one of the editors at Penguin – Udayan Mitra.

'I wrote these stories at different periods of my life. So sometimes they lack a connection. They are not written in a particular sequence, you know. Udayan thought it would be a good idea to bring them together in the order of sequence and give them a certain continuity so that the saga of Rusty can continue over three or four volumes. With his editorial help we've been putting them in order in which they might have happened, not in the order in which they're written.'

A: *'How many volumes have already been published?'*

RB: 'I think they have already published *Rusty: The Boy from the Hills*, *Rusty Runs Away*, and *Rusty and the Leopard*. Then there will be "Rusty No. 4", not to be confused with Rambo 1, 2, 3 and 4!'

A: *'The second volume of ghost stories edited by you has recently come out . . .'*

RB: 'Oh, that one I did for Rupa – *Ghost Stories from the Raj*. These are not my stories, which I put together. The first one I did—*The Penguin Book of Indian Ghost Stories*—was a mixture. They were old stories, which I had lying around with me for years, you know, in old magazines or collections. I thought it'd be a nice idea just to put them together.'

A: *'You yourself have written quite a few ghost stories. As a child you also read a lot of them. What really makes you go back to this genre again and again?'*

RB: 'Well, just half an hour before you phoned me, I might have had some thought transference from you, because I picked up an old volume – Algernon Blackwood (*Tales of the Uncanny and Supernatural*) . . . He was one of the classic writers. Blackwood is an old favourite of mine; he combines mysticism with the supernatural. He always appeals to me because there's a lot of mysticism and philosophy in it too. So that's true. I come back to ghost stories from time to time.'

A: *'Is Banaras Hindu University going to confer a D.Litt on you?'*

RB: 'Yes, but I've been hedging about, I'm such a lazy fellow, you know. To go wandering off to Banaras . . . I might lose my way! I don't know! But in any case, their convocation has been postponed for some time. So, there's still time for me to decide whether I should go and accept the honour or not.'

A: *'Did you get a letter from them? How did it happen?'*

RB: 'Just out of the blue. They wrote to me and said if I would like to accept D. Litt [*honoris causa* (Latin: for the sake of honour)]. I thanked them for the honour. But I said I was not sure if I could come at that particular time.'

A: *'You said elsewhere that since you didn't go to college, it (the D. Litt) would be something to write about.'*

RB: 'How to get a degree without going to college! It was a humourous comment. The fact that I didn't go to college was not that anyone prevented me; I could have gone. But I was quite a rebellious young man. And I wanted to start writing and earning a living straightaway. So I avoided going to college, you could say. But it seems colleges have not avoided me.'

A: *'Many intellectuals and discerning readers felt that the Padmoshri, which you were honoured with in 1999, should have come to you much earlier.'*

RB: 'I don't know. You see, I always lived a very low profile life. I never sort of try to push myself into the foreground of events and happenings . . . It took many years for me to become fairly well known as a writer. I also think that a lot of people were under the impression that I might be a foreign writer living in India. It's only gradually, over a period of time, that it has been accepted that I'm an Indian writer like any other Indian writer who uses English, and there's no shortage of them.

'I won't say it's (Padmoshri) belated. In fact, I'm surprised that I've got it at all! I'd not have been disappointed if I had not received Padmoshri/Sahitya Akademi or anything. That's because

I was certainly not expecting these honours or awards. . . .'

A: *'You had been to Bangalore sometime back?'*

RB: 'Yea, I did go to Bangalore a little over a year ago. I was invited by the Bangalore Golf Club to write a short history of the club, and something about Bangalore too. The book (*A Golf Story: Celebrating 125 years of the Bangalore Golf Club*) has just been published. This is not on general sale, except maybe in Bangalore. I enjoyed my stay there. They gave me a lot of material. It was my second visit to Bangalore after many years. It's a book about Bangalore, the way I see it and through the eyes of the Golf Club. It's basically for members—quite a decent production.'

A: *'Is it true that the owner of the Ivy Cottage (where Bond till recently had a rented accommodation) is going to sell the cottage?'*

RB: 'I bought my flat!'

A: *'You bought it?'*

RB: 'Yes.'

A: *'That's great news!'*

RB: 'But not the whole cottage or building, just this flat.'

A: *'When did it happen?'*

RB: 'Just a few months back. Yea, I finally bought it. It's not easy to find one, certainly not in Mussoorie. I know in an interview (published in *The Week*), I said something to the effect that I could not afford to buy it. But I managed to scrape enough together; and bought it.'

A: *'Not many people are aware that you've been writing for so long—for some fifty years now. You've struggled so much. How do you feel now?'*

RB: 'I was thinking the other day that it might be a good time now to write a little book of, may be, well, you could call it philosophy—my sort of outlook on my life as I've lived it. It's not just autobiography, but how I got through life without too many bruises. It could be a little bit of help to others may be. I could reflect on my writing career in it, try to put forward it as a simple homespun philosophy of living, which was never worked out in any deliberate way in my mind. It could be a mixture of Taoism & Thoreau's philosophy—bits and pieces of everything.'

As I pore over the transcript, news trickles in: There's going to be a sequel to *Ek Tha Rusty* (serialised on TV in the late nineties) to be telecast on DD Metro soon. So I ring up Assistant Director Tania Saili, daughter of the renowned travel writer and photographer Prof Ganesh Saili. 'Yea, we've already completed ten episodes of shooting based on Bond's novella *Who Killed the Rani* (being produced by Crown Communications),' says Tania, 'and submitted to the TV authorities. We're yet to receive the go-ahead. The matter is likely to be finalised in a month or so. Once the project is through, there will be more shoots (actor Ayub Khan plays the role of Rusty, Bond's alter ego) based on Bond's other novellas like *The Sensualist, Time Stops at Shamli, Love is a Sad Song. . . .*'

Inserting Poems in Prose Work: A Cunning Move!

The car trundles into the lawn of hotel Padmini Niwas at Library Stand, Mussoorie. As I clamber out of the car, I see that the mall wears a festive look: Bits of coloured papers are strung out overhead, all the way from near the famed Savoy Hotel to Picture Palace stand, along the entire length of the mall. A steady breeze has kept the paper festoons aflutter. Apart from the crowd making a beeline for the restaurants and shops lining the road, a loan mela is underway. SBI is doling out home loans on the street itself!

I'm on my way to conduct an interview with the first citizen of Mussoorie at about six in the evening. I beat on my hooves, past the *jhulaghar*, beyond the Cambridge & Chander bookshop, toward the Picture Palace; and then a sudden turn to the left leading to the Clock Tower, through the Landour Bazaar which is now geared to serving residents like Victor Banerjee and Pranoy Roy.

The Ivy Cottage nears. I feel my heart swell in anticipation of meeting up the author who is a household name in this part of the world and elsewhere. I am about to mount the steps that serve as a gangway between the mountain road and his cottage sitting pretty on top of a hill.

Ruskin Bond appears as if from nowhere, standing where the staircase levels up with the floor of the cottage. He watches me with an affectionate look as I pant my way up. He welcomes me saying, 'Always happy to see you!' Bond now owns this part of the Ivy Cottage, and shares it with his extended family. And whoever visits Bond, feels like a member of the family. Ruskin is as great a host as a writer. We converse animatedly for almost one-and-a-half hours.

A: *'Mulk Raj Anand, the father of Indo-English writing, used to like your soulful stories much; he also wrote articles extolling your work. Now that he is no more, do you wistfully remember Dr Anand who once paid you a visit?'*

RB: 'In fact I wrote about that visit in a recent book – *The India I Love*. It was a pleasant visit. He was full of life . . . That time he was already in his nineties. He had come here eight years ago to give a lecture at the academy.

'I think he was quite a formative influence on Indian writing in English . . . Someone writing novels in the forties (1940s) had to get published abroad. Here there wasn't the market, or any publisher who could give you some distribution and readership. So in a way, he was a pioneer.

'He had sympathy with the underdog, with the poorer, less privileged sections of society. I think his works deserve to be read still. I think publishers should make the effort to reprint some of his works which are not available easily, apart from the well-known ones like *Untouchable* and *Coolie* which are still in print. There are several others like *The Big Heart* or that autobiographical one *The Seven Summers* which is about growing up in Lahore. . . .'

A: *'You seem to have an affinity with Alfred Noyes, whose nature poems in particular seem to have influenced some of your prose pieces. For instance, your story "Binya Passes By" resembles, content-wise, Noyes' famous poem "Euterpe". Did you notice this?'*

RB: 'I have read Noyes as a boy, some of his poems. I read more of, you could say, (John) Masefield's poems. His poetry appealed to me. Also, Walter De La Mare, because nature is a part of many of his poems. So is the supernatural. They also appealed to me. I didn't read a great deal of Noyes. But I do remember some of his poems which have a good rhythm. For instance, his poem "Highwaymen". His story poems were also interesting.'

A: *'In* The Room on the Roof, *Rusty falls in love with Kishen's mother. Is it entirely a work of imagination? Or is there a grain of truth in it which is somewhat fictionalised to heighten the intensity of the story?'*

RB: 'Actually, I did have an infatuation for my friend's mother when I was sixteen or so. May be, in the fiction, in the process of writing the novel, I might have intensified it to give the story more strength and force. It's strange, you know, only the other day, since you ask me this question, a young teacher who is doing a Ph.D on my stories, asked me a question. He said, "Your love for Meena or for Binya or for Sushila—is it symbolic of your love or desire for union with India?" I have never thought of this. Ph.D. seekers dream up this sort of strange psychological association! I replied, "I never thought of that. Now that you mention it, well, why not, may be it was in the subconscious, the wish!"

'I only mention this because there is a similarity in the question pattern. Well, there was a kind of infatuation indeed . . . After all, there wasn't any future in it in having a crush on one's friend's mother! It happens to teenagers, you know. . . .'

A: *'Some of your poems and stories published in book-form have been wonderfully illustrated. You seem to have a passion for quality painting too. Who are your favourite painters? Do you find any connection between painting and writing?'*

RB: 'Well, painting and writing, both of them are forms of self-expression. I wish I could paint. Maybe that's why very often my nature writings are vivid and descriptive. It's very visual too. I never took any training in painting. I don't think I will do justice to my writing if I switch over to painting.

'Rabindranath Tagore is a great painter. I like the paintings of the French Impressionists like Monet, Renoir, also the English landscape painters like Turner and Constable. There are some great book illustrators also. I do appreciate good illustrations.

'When *The Room on the Roof* was first serialised in *The Illustrated Weekly of India*, Mario, who became quite famous as a cartoonist, illustrated it. He did some evocative illustrations. There is a cover of one of my books which I put there (on the wall of his study room). It's the cover for *Rusty: The Boy from the Hills* done by Tapas Guha. He has illustrated quite a few children's books. So did Suddha Satva. There have been others too.'

A: *'Do you suggest their names or does the publisher decide it?'*

RB: 'Once or twice I have suggested. In the case of Tapas Guha, I did. Otherwise the publishers often engage the illustrators. . . .'

A: 'The Diary of a Nobody *by Grossmith seems to be a favourite of yours. Particularly when in blue mood, this book, as you said elsewhere, always calms you down. Why do you think this book in particular never fails to bolster your spirit?'*

RB: 'I always found it very funny. It's very typical English humour. It always makes me laugh at myself; because it exposes the pomposity and self-importance of the main character in a way. It helps you to see the funny side of your own character, of one's own circumstances in life. I took myself too seriously when I was young, less seriously now.'

A: *'Does the act of writing help you form a shield against fear of old age, fear of death?'*

RB: 'I don't know whether it forms a shield. Maybe it helps towards an acceptance of death or whatever else there is. When I write, I sometimes become more conscious of the impermanence of things. But it can certainly help towards a philosophical acceptance of the limitations of life on this earth. So in that way, writing is certainly a good therapy, I think, for anybody. This is, I suppose, one reason why so many people keep diaries. It helps them even if they are not professional writers. It certainly helps them come to terms with their own selves. . . .'

A: *'Every writer has to deal with memory which, according to Conrad, is a painful business. Do you think so?'*

RB: 'It can be painful. I think, for Conrad, it would have been because he was so involved with his characters and people he had known. He was a person who grappled with life's problems. But most of us are selective in our memories, I think. We remember what we want to remember. We become nostalgic about the past because we are selective . . . We are inclined to blot out the more unpleasant memories which is just as well, otherwise if we carry traumas with us, we are going to have psychological problems sooner or later.

'I would not call memories a painful process. In fact, I enjoyed looking back and writing about people. Recently, I have been doing little character sketches called *Brief Lives* about people I have known. I'm just putting down what I remember about them; the kind of people they were, what impact they made, whether big or small on the world or those around them. And doing it is quite interesting. . . .'

A: *'You have won so many prestigious awards. Do they inspire you as a writer?'*

RB: 'I won't say they inspire me. But they might have given me some satisfaction of a feeling that somebody has recognised what little I have done and acknowledged in some way . . . As far as financial rewards go, they too helped me to continue writing and living life the way I wanted to. So they are welcome. I guess if they never come my way, I'd still be doing what I'm doing. But it's nice to have them.'

A: *'Once upon a time, through newspaper articles and stories, you used to bemoan the fact that very few journalists wrote on your literary output, that financially you were duped by some people who used your stories but paid you less than you deserved; and that financially it was somewhat frustrating for a writer to support himself entirely through writing. But those days are gone, thankfully. A lot of admirers are now beating a path to your door to meet you, to interview you, to work on you; and let me tell you that readers also love you as a thorough gentleman for your integrity and strength of character. I'm sure you also receive a lot of "fan" mail regularly; and pay a hefty amount of tax as well. Are you happy now? Do you see the hands of God in all this?'*

RB: 'It's a long and involved question. Thank you for the kind remarks you made. I can say I'm as happy now as I have ever been. I've always been a fairly optimistic or happy individual, even when times were not so good. You could say "content" would be a better word. It is true that about twenty or thirty years back it was very difficult getting books published in India. But that wasn't only my problem. I think any young writer at that time, you know, would have faced a similar situation. This is perhaps why many talented young writers, who were known to me, went into other professions or changed over to something else. Because they got discouraged from the fact that they could not make a living from their writings or maybe they encountered publishers who might have had their own problems and just collapsed.

'Publishing in India really came of age in the mid-eighties I think, and has since then gone from strength to strength; at least as far as general publishing goes. Because before that, there was a lot of academic publishing, you know, school books, textbooks . . . but as far as literature and other branches of writing are concerned, I think, it's only in the last ten or fifteen years that now a writer can get his work published and make a living and do reasonably well out of it. Many still aspire to be published in the West. Obviously, if you are published in the West, you are more widely known.

'My readership has always been here, basically. People do write to me and do often come to see me. It's gratifying that after so many years I've built up a readership . . . and they are fond of me too as a writer, which is a nice feeling indeed.

'You ended your question with "Do I see the hand of God in this?" Well, I'm not a very religious person; but you could say I'm a spiritual person. I have always seen the deity in the natural world around me, in nature and the things I love. So yes, perhaps, it's the hand of God that has sort of supported me or helped me along. But I have never thought of God in the conventional sense, in the sense of worship in a formal or any orthodox sort of system. I think, being a sort of nature worshipper, it has sustained me.

'What also sustained me is that although by nature I'm sensitive and impractical, I'm at the same time pragmatic. So I have always managed my work in such a way that I have lived within my means even when those means were not very substantial. When I look back on those earlier years, they don't seem difficult to me now, you know. Then, maybe, I felt insecure, and still do at times. But I think I was very fortunate. I did manage to continue doing what I loved doing, which was writing, and still making a viable living from it.'

A: *'During my meetings with Bill Aitken and Ganesh Saili, I got the impression that you are their literary mentor. Both of them admitted elsewhere their literary debt to you quite frankly. Do you think that a writer, when he has moved up a few steps on the ladder of success, should welcome new writings and new writers if they come along?'*

RB: 'Of course. One must welcome new writers. We're always new writers at some point in our lives.'

A: *'One doubts whether all writers welcome it!'*

RB: 'Well, I think, not all writers have a generosity of spirit. Very often, in the creative world, of not just writers, but also artists and musicians, you want to be the top man. But it seems so unnecessary to have that feeling, because, after all, no two writers are the same. It's really rare that two people are working on the same subject or theme or on the same lines. That can happen in a biography or history, but not in novel or poetry or writing of a very personal nature. And mine is very personal, since it is so much out of my own life; nobody else is going to write the same thing. So everybody is doing his or her own thing.

'Bill Aitken is a totally different kind of writer. He is a witty and clever travel writer. Ganesh Saili is more into journalism and photojournalism, when he is not teaching, of course. So they have all got their own different talents. I won't take credit for any of it. Except obviously if somebody comes to me and asks me for a suggestion or a bit of practical advice, I'll give it. It does not do me any harm. If I can do them any good, why not! I'd never discourage anyone from writing.

'But sometimes people, young or old, might turn up with a manuscript or a story or poetry. You read it and you see it's not very good. Then it is very hard because you don't know what to say. You don't want to discourage the person from writing. If you get pleasure from writing, you should write. At the same time, you want to warn them in a way and say that they might get disappointed if their novels or poems or things don't get published. You can't tell them it's sort of below par. It's a bit awkward sometimes.

'I would always say, "Well, if you enjoy writing, you must write. But don't expect to make a living from it or to become famous overnight". Sometimes young people do. They hear about writers like Arundhati Roy winning the Booker, and dream of becoming famous overnight. So they think that they can do the same! And they might be able to do the same. But it is not something you can just expect to happen every time you write a book. . . .'

A: *'Your biography by Ganesh Saili—*Ruskin, Our Enduring Bond*—hit the bookshops recently. . . .'*

RB: 'Well, it's largely a pictorial biography which has a lot of pictures from my own childhood. Then Prof Saili has quite a few pictures himself which he has taken over the years. And he has written a short text.'

A: *'Is it based on a series of interviews Prof Saili did with you?'*

RB: 'It's not based on any interview. It's just a chatty biography.'

A: *'Did he have access to your archives?'*

RB: 'It's based more on how he has known me over the years, you know, the last twenty or thirty years. There's another biography, based on archival materials plus all my work. This is done by Meena G. Khorana. She is a professor of English at Morgan State University. The book is called *The Life and Works of Ruskin Bond* (a literary biography of Ruskin Bond, Greenwood Publishing House). She got commissioned to do this. It's a university publication.'

A: *'The letters you exchanged with publisher Diana Athill bring out into sharp focus your seriousness of purpose as a writer at that tender age of seventeen or so. The inclusion of such letters was also a pleasant read for the would-be authors. Did you know then that these letters would some day form the part of your autobiography?'*

RB: 'No, I didn't know then. But I did preserve them, not realising that I would ever get to the point of writing an autobiography. Those letters were written in the fifties and the odd ones later on. Even a few months back she wrote to me. At one time I used to preserve interesting letters from interesting people; and still have a few. She was an important part of my early beginnings and early struggles as a writer, and gave me good advice. She is a friend too. It was only when I came to writing that autobiographical book—*Scenes from a Writer's Life*—that it occurred to me that the extracts can be included. Fortunately, I kept them.'

A: *'Do you think letter writing is one of the major art forms like stories and poems?'*

RB: 'It used to be. Now of course I think what happens is that fewer and fewer people are writing letters. In this computer age, people communicate more through e-mails or mobile phones. The art of letter writing, I'm afraid, is almost gone. Think of the letter writers of the eighteenth or the nineteenth centuries. Many of them are extant not only in museums but in books and biographies also. What care people took in writing their letters! I mean you could fill volumes with the letters of famous men and women, not just writers but in other walks of life too. I suppose people communicate so fast these days, through other means, that they don't bother to writer letters anymore.'

A: *'Artists are born sensitive. They get hurt so easily. And people sometimes make irresponsible comments. You must have been hurt by such comments before. What do you think should be the role of a responsible reviewer?'*

RB: 'It can't be helped . . . Occasionally you get odd bits of criticism which I think most writers are sensitive to. But we should also welcome criticism. Because after all you can't expect praise all the time; not everyone is going to like your work. So one should take it in one's stride and be philosophical. I hope the reviewer does not get personal. It's quite legitimate to say that you don't like a book and why you don't like it. But I don't think that the reviewers are being responsible if they make personal remarks about a particular writer saying, "Oh! He is an alcoholic! Or he is a philander!" They should concentrate on the work and say why they like or don't like it. That's what a critic is meant to do. A healthy literary climate also depends on good critics and reviewers, apart from the writers. Otherwise they are writing in a void, you know.'

A: *'You once said that you'd never be a poet because the last line of a poem always foxes you. Would you elaborate on this?'*

RB: 'I love writing poetry. I did some verses recently (published under the name *A Little Night Music* by Rupa & Co. in 2004). Whenever I get a chance, I sit down and write a few lines. The finishing of a poem is the most difficult part. I can make a good start, and get into the flow of it, and then perhaps I try too hard when I get to the end! So maybe one should just stop the poem halfway through! It should be more effective then! But I do enjoy writing poetry. And I wish I had written more. I hope I will, as time goes by. It's just that the publishers also have to sell your books. So they want you to write what you are known for . . . They expect more stories, novellas, or just entertaining essays. And poetry is hard to sell anyway, no matter who writes it. So I have to slip in the poems, here and there, in my prose works. You find odd poems cropping up in some of my books. That's a cunning move on my part!'

A: *'Anita Nair in* Outlook *(15 November 2004) writes: "On a rather distressing day while I was grappling with tax troubles, travel plans and several such irritants,* A Little Night Music*—a collection of verses by Ruskin Bond—arrived on my desk. Seeking distraction more than reprieve, I did a quick look-through and chanced upon one of* *the most delightful poems I have ever read – "All is Life". Perhaps it was how I was feeling then. Perhaps it was that there was a world of wisdom in that short poem. Perhaps it was the innate compassion that shone through. All poetry is subjective and it seemed as though the words spoke to me, me alone. 'Be Kind, my friend./Hold on, in times of pain and strife;/Until death comes, all is life. . . .'"*

Colleen and Hugh Gantzer wrote a wonderful article published in The Times of India *on your being awarded the Padmashri. Their travel writings are also of top quality. I try not to miss these worth-preserving articles published in* The Hindu *from time to time. Are you in touch with them?'*

RB: 'Yes, I am. In fact, only this morning I had a call from Hugh Gantzer in connection with the anecdotes I had written some time back on some interesting people who are buried in the Mussoorie cemetery. He is in charge of the cemetery. He wanted to know whether he could use them in some way in a leaflet or brochure about the cemetery. I said, "Of course, you can!" He travels a lot. We first met in around 1968-69. In fact, he grew up in Mussoorie as a boy and I only came to Mussoorie when I was thirty. By that time he was in the Indian Navy, and would then come on leave to Mussoorie. His mother was here. That's when we met for the first time. . . .'

Theme of Solitude

'Don't make it too long!' said Ruskin Bond over the phone in his baritone when I rang him up to say that I was in the process of doing a questionnaire based on his just published *Tales of the Open Road* (Penguin, 2006) and *Roads to Mussoorie* (Rupa, 2005). Despite my best efforts to keep the list short, I ended up asking some fairly long questions!

Bond does not type his stories anymore. He now writes in long hand; and his publishers prefer his hand written manuscripts! Needless to say, his handwriting is eminently readable.

Just a few years ago, Bond's monthly income from royalty was just a few thousands a month. At present, it is almost one hundred thousand a month. But during the last fifteen years or so, there was hardly any day when he was not besieged by visitors comprising students, would-be authors, journalists, honeymooners, and people from all walks of life from different parts of India and abroad.

Even now, once in a while, during his writing hours, he stays away from Ivy cottage at Landour, Mussoorie, where he resides with his extended family; and works at a haunted house which sits at a higher altitude than his Ivy Cottage. When I met Ruskin on 4 May 2006, he was reading a biography of his most favourite writer – Charles Dickens.

A: *'In a recent interview with Farrukh Dhondy, Nobel Laureate V.S. Naipaul praised unreservedly your autobiography* – Scenes from a Writer's Life. *He said there is one writer in India who could write so effectively about solitude without ever mentioning the word. How do you respond to that?'*

RB: 'Well, it's certainly very generous of him to praise that particular book of mine because he is not known to be over generous in his praise of writers in India and elsewhere. I have not read that complete article. Just the extract which appeared in *The Indian Express*, I think . . . Naturally, coming from him, it is nice to have that appreciation. I think I have written about solitude perhaps even more in other works of mine like *Rain in the Mountains*, or some of my autobiographical writing or fiction. In *Scenes from a Writer's Life*, what I was really trying to bring out was the loneliness of my childhood and boyhood. Perhaps that loneliness leads into the theme of solitude as well, because they are two different things really. Solitude is something that you choose; loneliness is a matter of circumstances. But I think it does come through that in the state of loneliness, one also learns the value of solitude. As Mr Naipaul says, it perhaps comes through in the book without being overstated.'

A: *'Any particular book by Naipaul you liked much?'*

RB: 'Well, right back in the fifties I read his first book which was his collection of stories – *Miguel Street*. The reason I did so was that a year after I won the John L. Rhys prize, which was in 1957, he received the same award for *Miguel Street* (in 1958). Of course, our path has never crossed; we have never met each other. But he was also one of André Deutsch's first writers, you know. He went on to write other books for André Deutsch after *Miguel Street* . . . Then of course you had *A House for Mr Biswas* and other books set in the West Indies, where he grew up. What he might have in common with me is that he too was growing up in an environment which was not of his choice but where his parents and grandparents had settled. Originally, they had come from India. My parents and grandparents had come from England and settled in India. So I was also growing up in an environment which was not originally of my choice but to which I adapted and made my own. So perhaps, that was something that might have touched a chord with him too. I think he would be about my age or may be a year or two older.'

A: *'While describing your journey to Kedarnath and Badrinath (as reminisced in* Tales of the Open Road, *Penguin, 2006), you often talked about the sacred river Ganges. In fact, you spent a night by the river just to listen to the sounds of it. Do you think sounds of the water falling over a rock or cascading down a range can heal a world-weary soul?'*

RB: 'Sounds, I think, are underestimated. Certain sounds are disturbing or troublesome or would do the opposite of healing to a world-weary soul. Others are soothing sounds like birdsong or crickets or insects singing. Sounds of water are usually soothing, the water running over shingle or waves lapping on a beach, if you're near the sea. All these natural sounds do have healing effects. And some sounds stand out because they take place in silence very often. In the middle of the night, when all is still and quiet, and you hear the little nibbling of a mouse, or the lizard scuttling about, these sounds stand out and take on added significance in a way.'

A: *'Are you actually very fond of cheap metal rings which you bought in pocketfuls in Badrinath?'*

RB: 'Oh well, my friends tease me that I get taken in by glitter. So I am like a raven who likes to collect these little baubles, but only briefly. Because as soon as I got back from Badrinath, I gave away all these rings and trinkets and little things to the kids and to anybody who wanted it. It's a sort of brief moment of madness, you could say.'

A: *'Do you still chance upon some beautiful wild flowers by the hillside? Are their numbers decreasing by the day?'*

RB: 'Well, wild flowers are always there. But true, sometimes you find that a certain flower or species of flowers have vanished from a particular area for various reasons. Maybe climatic reasons or the road is being built or because of diesel fumes from passing traffic. But you will find them elsewhere. Only the rarer species would perhaps be going extinct. Otherwise the most common wild flowers can still be found somewhere or the other.'

A: *'Can you name some?'*

RB: 'Yes, well, I will tell you what would be out in this particular month (May). You will get the St. John's Wort. This is a wild flower common to England and Europe as well. It's like a shrub on the hillside. It has got yellow flowers. In the old days, there was a belief that if you keep these flowers beneath your pillow, they will keep away evil spirit. That's quite common up here. Then you get the Mayflower which, as its name implies, flowers in May. Also, at this time of the year, a lot of daisies grow on the hillside. The Iris has also spread and sort of gone wild up here. There is also the dog rose, the wild rose.'

A: *'Why it is called dog rose?'*

RB: 'I will tell you why. Because back in Europe, in the middle ages, it was given as an antidote for dog bite. So these are a few for the month of April and May only. They will vary from month to month.'

A: *'At the outset of* Roads to Mussoorie *(Rupa, 2005), you inform the reader of "a haunted house on Tehri road" where you work these days. Is it because of the steady stream of visitors who keep coming to your Ivy cottage at Landour at odd hours unannounced that you felt the necessity of a hangout hidden away from the reach of the casual visitors?'*

RB: 'Well, you come announced. But a lot of people do come unannounced! I will tell you the truth about the haunted house. I have been there off and on. I don't go there regularly. But if I am enjoying my afternoon siesta, say between 2.00 pm to 4.00 pm, then I leave word with family members that if anybody comes unannounced, they should tell them that they will find me at the haunted house! So they can have a long walk; they may not find it. But certainly, they won't find me! But usually I am quite happy to see visitors if they give me some warnings. I used to go to the haunted house when I lived higher up the hill which was closer to the house. The house still exists. It's still in ruins. It has not been occupied. I have been there quite a few times but have not seen the ghost! There are jackals living there now. Occasionally, a leopard too. Once I saw it crossing the road. But the leopard will not attack or be aggressive. Only if you have a dog with you, he might seize the dog.'

A: *'Of all places that you've trekked over the years, Nandprayag happens to have a specicl niche in your heart. For here you felt as if you had been in this lush green and river-threaded valley in your previous life. Could you please throw some light on this strange feeling you had which surely borders on the mystical?'*

RB: 'It's a feeling that I had been there before. All of us occasionally get this feeling of having been in a place before, a feeling of deja-vu. It does not happen very often; happens very rarely in fact. I had never been to Nandprayag before. But when I did—I only spent a day and a night there—it seemed so familiar to me as if I had been there perhaps in a dream state on in some other existence.'

A: *'It's amazing to know that you used to travel, when you were younger, the distance between Rajpur in Dehra to Mussoorie by walking! These long walks along the steep terrain provided you with subjects for the timeless stories you penned. Just like letter-writing, walking too has now become a thing of the past. When you visit the famous Savoy Hotel, do you at times walk all the way from your cottage?'*

RB: 'I used to. The old footpath was only seven miles from Rajpur to Mussoorie . . . Now I don't go because the Savoy Hotel has been sold. It's being pulled down to be restored. Hopefully it will open again next year.'

A: *'Is Nandu the manager of Savoy, whom you wrote about, still here?'*

RB: 'No! He lives in Bangalore now. He comes occasionally; because he has kept his cottage on the estate. At the moment Savoy is closed for renovation.'

A: *'You still walk as you used to?'*

RB: 'Not as much. I have some gout problems these days. It has restricted the walking to a considerable extent. But I still do walk. I walked up to the top of the hills last week, but far more slowly than I used to.'

A: *'Certain flesh and blood characters continue to crop up in almost whatever you write – your dear father and your dear lady-friend, Sushila (not the real name I suppose). As* Roads to Mussoorie *nears the end, you devote a glowing paragraph to your romantic friendship with this lovely lady who must be above sixty now. The readers wonder sometimes – did she ever read the stories you dedicated to her? Or does she know that now you're such a celebrated writer?'*

RB: 'Yes! She does know!'

A: *'She knows?'*

RB: 'She knows that I am quite well-known now; I don't know if she reads the stories. She probably used to read in Hindi more than in English. Now that some of the books have been translated into Hindi, she might have come across them. She knows that I am quite well-known.'

A: *'How do you know that she knows?'*

RB: 'Well, she is being in touch, lately, not so long ago. There is also a story in a sequel about her, not published in any other book. It's in a collection called *Rupa Book of Indian Love Stories* published about a year back. It's about meeting her again after some twenty or thirty years. It's quite a humourous story.'

A: *'It was such a lovely story, the first one on Sushila . . . It's something great. The relationship is still intact even after almost forty to fifty years.'*

RB: 'You are probably referring to "Love is a Sad Song" and "Time Stops at Shamli". She comes in that again. Then she is mentioned in *Funny Side Up*, which has just been published. There in a chapter called "Whatever happened to Romance", I have written about her in a piece called "Love and Cricket" . . . Yes, she telephones me. . . .'

A: *'If I may ask you, your income from royalty in recent times has considerably gone up. It's reported in the Outlook. . . .'*

RB: 'She (the reporter) made a mistake there or they made a mistake in printing. When she asked me how much I earned five or ten years back, I did not say three to four hundred rupees as is printed there. I said three to four thousand; the former is correct as applying to the 1950s when I started freelancing. She got it mixed up. It has gradually gone up with the passage of time.'

A: *'Is it true that you are earning about eighty thousand to one lakh rupees a month at present?'*

RB: 'Yes, over the last few years it has worked out to this amount.'

A: *'You must be paying a hefty income tax as well?'*

RB: 'Yes I do. You know, up to three lakhs of your income on royalty is exempt from tax. A writer can also claim a lot of expenses such as secretarial/postage/typing/travel—anything connected with one's work. There also used to be an exemption on income earned from abroad; that has gone now. Then, senior citizens also get a fairly good exemption; it has gone up to a lakh. I use a Chartered Accountant; he submits the return of my accounts and claims various things. Then it is up to the assessment officer to decide on what I should and should not pay.'

A: *'Have you stopped typing altogether?'*

RB: 'Almost. Because I started getting a stiff neck from typing; and probably would with a computer too. I am writing by hand now. Since my handwriting is neat and readable, the publishers don't mind. My last two or three books (manuscripts) have all been handwritten. Only for something very official I might use my typewriter.'

A: *'Any new book forthcoming?'*

RB: 'Penguin is now planning a book about my Dehradun writing, the stories or essays that were based on or set in Dehradun. It is to be called *A Town Called Dehra*. This will hark back to the Dehradun of 1940s and '50s. I will do an introduction comparing the Dehradun of yesteryears and today so that the reader will not think: "Look, this place does not exist!" To tell you the truth, I am on strike now! For a week or two. Then I will get back to work.'

The Greatness of Ruskin Bond

An Interview with the Author of
Creative Contours of Ruskin Bond:
Dr Prabhat K. Singh

The Greatness of Ruskin Bond

Where does the actual credit of a creative writer lie? Is it in the self-conscious attempt to idiomatise the write-up, to choose specifically those words which are not oft-used, or to give too much attention to the shape and ring of each and every sentence?

Or, is it in the writer's ability to evoke sympathy in the heart of the reader through a particular style of writing? A style which befits the content and which shuns the tendency to impress—by ferreting out phrases which could well be done without—for the sake of greater clarity?

Those who have read Ruskin Bond know for sure that he is supremely gifted, for he possesses an uncanny innate power to move the reader. Such is his magnetic personality that no reader of Bond could possibly brush his stories aside half-read. Yet he has been pilloried and tomahawked by some critics who once thought him fit only to be published in weekend supplements as his style of writing, according to them, is very 'simple'.

Bond takes up this issue in the introduction to his *Best of Ruskin Bond*:

'People often ask me why my style is so simple. It is, in fact, deceptively simple. It's clarity that I'm striving to attain, not simplicity. Of course, some people want literature to be difficult. And those who think this is simple should try it for themselves.'

Although many readers, scholars and critics have expressed their greatest admiration for Bond down the years, it is Dr Prabhat K. Singh, professor of English at Gaya College, a creative writer himself, who for the first time realised the long felt need to publish all the writings done so far on Bond in book form. It was a mammoth task. Dr Singh pulled all the stops out and his genuine love for Bond carried him through. Finally, after two years of vigorous research, his dream came true. The book, *The Creative Contours of Ruskin Bond,* finally got published in 1995.

Excellently edited and introduced by Dr P.K. Singh, this anthology of critical writings on Bond has been hailed by Bond enthusiasts all over the world. The list of contributors includes writers like Mulk Raj Anand, Bill Aitken, Ganesh Saili, Victor Banerjee, Sudhir Thapliyal, P. Lal, Dilip Bobb, Meena G. Khorana, the editor himself, and many others. I met Dr Singh at Gaya College and conducted the interview at his residence which is a short walk away from the college.

Author: *When and how did he fall in love with the stories of Bond?*

P.K. Singh: 'Oh, that was some fifteen years back. It so happened that one day a student came to me with *The Room on the Roof* in his hand. He wanted me to discuss that book. So, I went through it. And I liked it very much. That was how I got initiated into the world of Bond. And I decided to read other works of Bond.'

A: *Did the novel strike him in any special way?*

PKS: 'Two things, mainly. The way he traces the growth of a child and how innocence is exposed to certain facets of life. That adds to the very seriousness of life. And his prose is crystal clear and the narrative pattern straight, not much complex. With little number of words he creates deep effects.'

A: *How did* The Creative Contours of Ruskin Bond, *the only one of its kind, come about?*

PKS: 'A full-length work on him was lingering in my mind for some time. It was not occupying the centre of my consciousness, but then it was moving on the periphery. And then it gripped me like a demon, almost. I went on writing letters to most of the people I knew and I circulated the news through many literary journals. Fortunately, I got a very warm response. That way, you know, I could give the whole historicity to Bond criticism.'

A: *When did he write his first letter to Bond?*

PKS: 'It was on 21 November 1993. And Mr Bond was very kind in his reply. He wrote, "Sorry for the delay in replying to your kind letter. I was out of Mussoorie for some time. I'm enclosing some reviews. Iswar J. Taki wrote a thesis on my work and you might ask her to contribute to the book. You might also like to write to Bill Aitken. And to Jaishankar Kala who is in Hampstead, London".'

A: *Did Bond like the anthology?*

PKS: 'Very much. He was happy with the quality of the production, with the comprehensive nature of its material. In another letter he wrote, "It was very gratifying to see and go through the anthology."'

A: *His Hindi translation of Bond's* Strangers in the Night *has been published by Atmaram, New Delhi. Why did he choose this book out of all the books by Bond?*

PKS: 'When *Strangers in the Night* was brought out by Penguin India separately, Bond sent me a copy as a gift. As I read along, I found a new kind of flavour in his writing. The immense translatability of the book struck me.

'*The Sensualist* was banned in the seventies. So there was also the commercial viability of the book. Finally, it was my intention to show that Bond is not a children's writer first, but that he can handle expertly, complex realities like sex as well.'

A: *Grapevine has it that he is already flooded with the requests to translate Bond's other stories into Hindi. How far has he been successful in translating Strangers in the Night into Hindi?*

PKS: 'While translating, I tried to preserve the actual wavelength of the writer as far as possible. However, when I sent the manuscripts to Raj Kamal Prakashan in Delhi, they opined that my language was elite, not the common diction of the masses. I did find some substance in the comment and re-did the manuscripts, in parts. Translation is like a woman – if faithful not beautiful and if beautiful, not faithful! Yes, I've some offers on hand.'

Perhaps the highest praise came from Bill Aitken, the renowned travel writer. In a letter addressed to Dr Singh, Aitken summed up his achievement thus:

'. . . I thought you'd be coming to Mussoorie to meet Ruskin . . . you've not only enabled Ruskin to be viewed as a respectable figure amongst academics but redeemed the reputation of Magadh. Frankly, I'm amazed at your industry and organisation to achieve, according to the schedule, a book of such appealing standards.'

The Creative Contours of Ruskin Bond (Pencraft, New Delhi) is admirably produced. For scholars working on Bond and for his countless readers, the book is an absolute must. The book happens to be the maiden attempt to do justice to the genius of Bond, an exceptional artist who writes for soul's sake. Unjustified criticism, if there be any, does not disconcert him any more. 'The bright lights', says Bond, 'whether in the circus or on the film sets, were not for me. The writer's art is a lonely one.'

Tania Saili on Ruskin Bond
NDTV 24x7, Uttaranchal Bureau
Trim Lodge, Mussoorie

'Longevity is the only real test of good literature.'

Author: *'When was your first brush with Ruskin Bond's work?'*

Tanya Saili: 'I have known Ruskin Bond as a friend of the family since I was a child. I have read his work for over sixteen years now.'

A: *'Is there any story by Bond which still stands out in your memory?'*

TS: '"The Eyes Have It".'

A: *'What exactly is it in Bond's stories that you think appeals to Indian readers at large?'*

TS: 'Ruskin Bond's stories are written for Indian readers without an eye on an international audience. He writes about India for Indians. Hence there is no glorification of poverty, no slickness, no smugness. There is no artifice to his works, it is written from the heart.'

A: *'Have you ever recommended any book by Bond to anyone?'*

TS: 'Of course. I have to recommend it to anyone who likes to read good literature—for I believe that there is essentially no difference between those who do not read and those who cannot read.'

A: *'How do you find Ruskin Bond as a person?'*

TS: 'Ruskin Bond is the gentlest of human beings, kind and

tolerant to almost any fault. He is forever encouraging, those whom he knows, to write and be creative.'

A: *'Where do you place Bond in the canon of Indian writing in English?'*

TS: 'Among the canons (are there really that many?) of Indian writing in English, he is way ahead of others who bask in the media hype. His work will be read long after all of us are gone, long after today's plastic heroes crumble in the dust of time. For longevity is the only real test of good literature.'

A Short Story Dedicated to Ruskin Bond

'*I* read your story "Birth of a Poem" and it brought back the pangs of desire that once seized—but now only mock—this ageing body. The style in places is reminiscent of Ruskin (Bond).'

—Bill Aitken

'"Birth of a Poem" is a highly readable story.'

—Manoj Das

'Your story "Birth of a Poem" is typical of your own self – subjective, lyrical, soft and personal.'

—Prof (Dr) Kuntal Chattopadhyay

Birth of a Poem

I was on my way to Landour to do an interview with my favourite writer. I might never have wanted to visit the place had I not fallen head over heels in love with the stories set on and around the mysterious Malgudi-like towns such as Dehra, Pipalnagar, Shamli, etc., created by the author I was dying to meet.

At the Delhi bus stand, as I hopped onto a Dehradun-bound private bus, I found two foreigners, both of them ladies, talking to each other in English. They happened to be sitting in the back row, just beside my seat. In spite of my lack of fluency in their language, I got on well with them particularly from the moment we learnt that all three of us had been overcharged some hundred rupees or so!

To alleviate my sense of loneliness a bit, I told them I was going to meet a celebrated writer, the creator of the unforgettable character – Rusty. They asked me whether I was carrying any of his books with me. 'Yes', I said, 'I have quite a few of his books with me right now. Would you like to have a look at them?'

They seemed genuinely interested. One of them introduced herself, 'I'm Sylvia from Scotland. She is Nicole, my companion, a painter from America. I teach English and French in a school at Oxford. Both of us are lovers of art and literature. Could you choose a story of him for us? We would like to read it right here and now.'

The American lady showed me some of the sketches she had done in Delhi and Agra. I found that she was very fascinated, particularly by the dome-shaped buildings, and was able to capture the spirit of silence and loneliness through such paintings.

When I asked them to read, 'What's your dream', a story by the writer I was ordained to meet, Sylvia, the teacher, read it aloud. The stray conversations within the moving bus and the noise pouring in from outside posed no problem for them. The story was barely two pages long. When she finished reading it, they seemed to have liked it much. They immediately asked me the titles of some of the books by the same author which I supplied without much ado. And we talked on with intervals of lingering silence.

It was getting dark when the bus pulled up at Haridwar. Mussoorie was still a few hours away. I decided to break the journey there. Sylvia and Nicole were Rishikesh-bound; so all three of us got down at Haridwar.

My discovery of Haridwar was a by-product of travelling to Landour, for my original plan was to go to Mussoorie directly from New Delhi. However, as Haridwar approached, the light steadily waned. On an impulse born out of the fact that I was a complete stranger in that part of the world, I decided to stay overnight at Haridwar before resuming the journey to Landour next morning. So it was not pre-planned. Now, looking back, I realise as to why the power we call destiny made me spend a few hours at the holy place in the fleeting company of a strangely beautiful woman.

My first visit to the holy city of Haridwar was like falling in love for the first time. From the bus stand, we took a ride in the rickshaw as the western horizon smeared with crimson streaks of fleecy clouds began to cast its magical spell on the ashrams, hotels and the streets. We put up at a nearby *dharmshala*, much to the chagrin of the rickshaw puller who spoke English fairly well and did his best to persuade the foreigners to check into a plush hotel.

Whatever hotel or holiday home I stay in when I reach the destination, there is always a secret, overwhelming longing to go to the topmost floor or the roof of the building to have a sweeping view of the surrounding scapes. Such a view always helps me keep myself at a distance from the turmoil outside.

So, immediately after noting the time of our arrival in the register provided by the caretaker (who looked visibly pleased to have foreign tourists), I went straight to the roof taking along Sylvia and Nicole. One could see from the rooftop the mushrooming of hotels and ashrams. What struck me most was the Maa Mansa Devi temple perched on the Sivalik mountain range. The tiny lights on the temple had just been lit. It seemed so near from the dharmshala. The encroaching darkness dotted with winking lights all around with the brightly lit temple atop the Bilwa Parvat, raised in me a sense of gratitude for being alive. My newly found friends were also very excited, it seemed. 'Sylvia', I said, 'When you wake up in the morning, let's go to the temple together.' She looked at me with her eyes smiling but said nothing.

Before long, we were ambling off down the path leading to the famed Har ki Pauri bridge that spans the holy Ganges, the centre of all activities.

It was a full moon night. The water of the sacred river, perpetually running in one direction, was sparkling with the silvery moonlight. The wind was rather chilly. Nicole was not in a mood to walk around. Her gout was giving her trouble, she said. She sat by the riverside while Sylvia and I decided to take a stroll along the bridge. The sound of the gong was in the air as the Ganga *aarti* had just started.

I liked Sylvia more than Nicole particularly because she spoke chaste English as well as French; also because she had an air of aloofness around her which was hard to define. I often found her going into her shell. It was Nicole who took it upon herself to cheer her up whenever she looked a bit distraught. During the journey by bus, Nicole once playfully scolded her for looking depressed and asked for my support, 'Is there any use taking life so seriously? Should one not take things as they come?' Then I instinctively knew something was troubling Sylvia.

As we strolled on to the other side of the river I asked her, 'Your friend and you have some common traits. Both of you love silence. She is a painter; so are you. But she says she often finds you lost in deep thought, completely unaware of the movable feast around you. Is that true?'

'I don't know', said she, 'We're very close. We have come here in search of peace. By nature I'm an introvert. I often go into depression. Nicole sort of buoys me up, tries her best to put cheerfulness into my sagging soul.' She fell into silence.

The cold was bone-chilling. As we slowly walked, our bodies, now and then, came very close and touched lightly. She was very young. Her mass of hair was gathered and done up in a heap on top of her head. She wore a jeans and a jumper that accentuated her firm breasts. Back on the Har ki Pauri bridge, she opened her mouth again. 'I'm alone now. I can't sleep at night. During daytime I teach at school, remain too busy with children. Back home I do my painting. But as the night-time approaches, all hell breaks loose. My past catches up with me.' She then took out a diary from her bag and showed me, in bright moonlight, a photo of a man who was of strong build. He sported long hair but before I could draw any conclusion whether it's the man she broke up with, she abruptly put the diary back in her bag and closed off the conversation adding, 'I have my friends. We keep in regular touch.'

We could see Nicole beckoning furiously. Obviously she was getting impatient. We had been walking together for barely half an hour. Since our arrival at Haridwar, we had not had anything to eat; we were really hungry. Dada Boudi's hotel was just a few minutes' walk from Har ki Pauri. The hotel, famous for its quality Bengali vegetarian food at a rather cheap rate, was not crowded at that hour in the evening. Sylvia and Nicole sat on the same side facing me. It was a treat to watch them having rice and sabji with gusto. We all had a ravenous appetite. The piping hot food worked wonders on our psyche. It was about eight when we finished our dinner. The cold outside was indeed too much to bear. We went straight back to the dharmshala. 'Remember Sylvia', I said, before turning in, 'We're going to the temple tomorrow.'

However much I tried, I could not sleep that night for a long time. Whatever direction I looked, there was the image of Sylvia. The chemistry between us worked for a while. I wanted the night to end there and then. My mind, despite myself, kept going back to the stroll we had together. I did not know when sleep overtook me. When I woke up I saw a shaft of sunlight slicing across my bed. I jumped out of the bed and dashed out of the room only to find their room under lock and key. They had gone out.

My heart sank. For all my maturity gained through strict self-discipline, I could not help feeling depressed. I hit the road immediately. On my way to the temple, every few minutes, I stopped and scoured the shops and the streets looking for them. They were nowhere to be found. There were too many devotees at the temple. One could hear the bhajan being aired from the temples on the nearby hilltop. There was a distinct sense of purity and freedom in the air. But my sinking feeling persisted. Within a few hours I was supposed to catch hold of a Dehradun-bound bus on my way to Mussoorie. I returned to the dharamshala to pack my things up.

Half an hour later, I heard footsteps on the stairs. I heard the sounds of the key turning in the lock in the room Sylvia and Nicole were occupying. My heart started throbbing furiously. I deliberately let a few minutes drop by before stepping into their room. Sylvia was seated alone on the narrow bed. When asked, I sat on the edge of her bed. The early morning chill had brought out the rosy tints on her cheeks. I did not ask why they had not taken me with them. What I did ask was how they enjoyed their morning out in an unknown place like Haridwar, unguided.

'You could say', she said, 'we did a little bit of trekking, following the trail of the holy river. On our way, we came to a point under a bridge, where I found that the chortling sound of the water had a particular rhythm—now a sibilant whisper, now breaking out in a soft loud gurgling before going back to the state of murmuring. I stood there rooted, sensing a calmness descending upon my fragile heart as never before. Could you guess what I did then? I recorded the sound of the water!' She then played the cassette for me to listen to the mysterious sound of the running water. While listening to it, I felt my scalp bristling and goose pimples erupting all over my body.

'I'm sure you will take it back to your country so that you can listen to it whenever you feel low.'

'No! I'll leave it behind! Out of Haridwar, it's unlikely to have any effect on me.'

'Are you sure?'

'Yes, absolutely.'

'Then give it to me!'

As I said this, her smile suddenly disappeared. Her face took on a sombre expression. She refused to make any eye contact with me. After a few moments of unbearable silence, she carelessly threw the cassette on a nearby table and said in a grave tone, 'I don't know what to do with it. Let me think over.' Obviously, she was not willing to part with it. But the tone of her voice stung me to the quick.

At this point, Nicole came in and immediately broke the silence by announcing that all of us should visit the Har ki Pauri market on the Vishnu Ghat Road and the adjoining areas as she had some urgent purchases to make. This time I accompanied them. The sky was a bit cloudy. The maze of lanes crisscrossing the market was crowded at this hour of the morning. None of us uttered a word as we negotiated the swelling crowd. Just as we came near the bank of the river, where the evening aarti was being performed the day before, Nicole handed me her Nikon camera; she asked me to photograph them, and told me where to click.

As I was adjusting the angle through the viewfinder and trying to get the heaving hills as the backdrop, there came a sudden pelting rain. Somehow I handed back the camera to Nicole, and we all ran helter-skelter for shelter. It was a short but fierce rain, lasting only a few minutes. When it let up as abruptly as it came, there was no sign of either Nicole or Sylvia. I cast my glance in all directions, but to no avail. They had simply vanished. After exploring the market for half an hour, all alone, I returned to the dharmshala. The caretaker seemed surprised to see me. 'Your friends have just left for Rishikesh,' he said. 'Would you join them later?' Something snapped in me again. Being in a tearing hurry for spiritual succour, they had no time to bid me goodbye. I somehow managed to bring a forced smile to my lips and went to my room.

It was almost noon when I clambered aboard a Mussoorie-bound bus, my mind in complete disarray. However, as the journey progressed, my only passion in life to be face to face with the revered writers gradually survived the haunting memories of Sylvia. I reasoned that the episode was only 'an incident in the passion and not the cause of it' (courtesy Gertrude Stein). I remembered that I had sent a published article on his love stories to the author along with a letter requesting him for a heart to heart exchange. And I received the letter of my life.

But no editor had commissioned me to interview him. I was not in mainstream journalism, just a hapless freelancer, virtually unknown, whose articles got published only once in a blue moon. Now a new tension took hold of my heart – what if he was out of station? Suppose he would not consent to be interviewed? Most of the passengers had dozed off, swaying with the zigzag motion of the bus. I stayed awake, constantly remembering the soul-stirring lines from his stories I had memorised with avidity. I had also prepared a list of questions which I kept rehearsing.

The first thing I did after reaching Mussoorie was to give the author a ring. No, he was not at home. There was a loud thud against my ribs. Was he out of his hometown? No! He had gone to the Landour market. My heart started beating again. Next time I phoned, it was the author himself who picked up the receiver. Oh, what a thrill it was—talking over the phone to the master storyteller whose books you had been reading for over a decade and came to identify yourself so many times with the characters he fashioned out with such a rare sensitivity.

Next day the interview lasted for an hour. He never once asked which paper I was representing. Nor did he ask to see the write-up before publication. Some critics opine that you should be interested only in the works of the author, but not in meeting the writer in flesh and blood. However, later, much later, I was to discover that authors, almost without exception, always took a special liking to someone who had gone through their works diligently and liked them, no matter whether he/she was a journalist by profession or not. And meeting a gifted writer was indeed a great feeling. I felt the way Kipling did when he met his favourite writer Mark Twain.

Meeting the author of my choice immediately after this strange happening helped me to square with my ruffled conscience. But back home, the experience was still catching my heart at random till I actually sat down to write, armed with the cassette holding the conversation with my favourite writer. Needless to say, the idea of the poem never occurred to me when I was undergoing the pain of unceremonious separation from Sylvia.

The birth of a poem is a very painful process. One has to undergo a great deal of heartache trying to mine buried memories and then sculpt it in the shape of words on the white canvas. But once you exactly follow the systole and the diastole of the heart's utterance, there's a sense of exhilaration, which again washes over the author when it is published!

The theme of the poem was Sylvia's interest in the sound of the water hurtling down the craggy, rugged slope of the mountain, and then moving at a furious speed along the sloping riverbed dotted extravagantly with huge boulders against which the plunging onrushing water cavorted and played with a wild abandon before running on. For me too, it has always been music to a tired, world-weary soul. I dwelt on that and purged the poem of the humiliation I had felt. I actually extolled her for such a wonderful idea—the idea of recording the soothing sound of running water, before allowing the reader a peep, somewhat obliquely, into my aching soul. I must confess that the poem took a life of its own without my realising it.

When I submitted both the poem and the interview to the editor of a national daily, he was visibly impressed with the interview. He did not care to have a look at the poem but accepted it all the same. Surprisingly, he published the poem first, before according the interview, as he said, to its rightful place—'The Middle'—a couple of months later. The poem was superimposed on a beautiful computerised illustration, more eloquent than the poem. It showed the flowing river with boulders on its bed and diyas floating on its surface, and a face—lovely yet sorrow-laden—of a lady looking at the reader with her 'opal eyes' from under the crystal clear water. Strangely again, the face resembled the face of Sylvia!

It does not hurt me anymore when I recall how Sylvia refused to part with the cassette. Perhaps I should not have asked for it in the first place. Also, it did not occur to me then that I could have recorded some such sound myself at Haridwar. But the sound that emanated from Sylvia's cassette still rings in my ears. It will probably never leave me. These days, whenever I get any blues, I have only to concentrate on this ethereal sound for a while. And lo, I'm my usual self again.

(Published in *The Asian Age* Festival Issue & in
The Journal of Literature & Aesthetics)

Letters from Ruskin Bond

To the Author...

28 May 1995

Dear Mr Banerjee,

It was very kind of you to send me your article on my love stories, otherwise I would probably have missed it. It's a perceptive and finely-written piece. Thanks!

Do send me your questionnaire; I'll be out on a trek during the next two weeks, so end of June will be best.

Can you recommend a love story by a Bengali writer (in English or English translation) which I could include in a Penguin India anthology of Indian love stories? Something written this century. . . .

Warm regards,
Ruskin Bond

5 August 1995

Dear Swapan Kumar,

My apologies for taking so long to reply to your letters. The past month has been rather crowded. Thanks for sending me the questionnaire and the story. I'll get around to them at the first opportunity. I have been besieged by visitors in recent months—can't do any serious work—sometimes I wish I was the unknown writer of thirty years ago, when I could compose my stories and vignettes without interruption!

Will be in touch soon.

Yours,
Ruskin Bond

5 December 1997

Dear Mr Swapan Banerjee,

Many thanks for your letter and for sending me copies of *Calcutta Plus*. It was good to see your interviews—I shall keep it for my archives! I liked your poem (published in *The Economic Times*)—will keep that too!

We have had some severe cold weather and early snowfall. The memoir is now out (*Scenes from a Writer's Life*), and I have started work on the second volume. I hope you will write many good articles and poems during the coming months. My very best wishes to you. . . .

Sincerely yours,

Ruskin Bond
Landour, Mussoorie.

Dear Swapan Banerjee,

Your kind letter of 22 December took some time getting here—over a month—due to the rather ragged condition of the postal service at present.

I had no idea that I had any gifts as a speaker—I do my best to avoid getting up on a rostrum even if it's only to avoid saying a few words! But I do unwind a little on a person-to-person basis.

Thank you for your kind wishes for 1998, which I sincerely reciprocate.

Yours,
Ruskin Bond

5 April 1998

Dear Swapan,

Your kind letter and the articles — thanks very much. Your earlier letter was sent on to Dr Gotlieb, as I thought he would appreciate it. I will also send him copies of your reviews/interviews.

Good luck with your thesis on Conrad's influence on Jack London.

After a long drawn-out winter, we are finally getting a few warm and sunny days.

Every good wish,
Ruskin Bond

Poem

'Always good to hear from you. Thanks for your deeply-felt poem.'

—Ruskin Bond in a letter dated 27 October 2001

Ruskin Bond

Ivy cottage at Landour, Mussoorie,
The retreat of the writer—
The chipped and worn look of it—
Provides you some clue
About his magnanimity,
About his complete unconcern
Of all earthly possessions.

Fatherless at ten
And deprived of motherly affection
At an even earlier age
When his parents separated,
His ESP confirmed
There was in him
A writer in the making.
There was practically no one then
Who understood him.

His adventurous and fearless spirit
Drew him to the splendours
Of the Kalpi-like hamlets
Cradled in the bosom
Of Garhwal mountains.

He observed with great clarity
The Indian way of life
Particularly in the mountainous regions
And wrote about it with an élan
One generally associates with writers
Like Kipling, Noyes, Chekhov . . .

Not many artists had to face
What he did.
All along, he was ready to trade anything
To safeguard his freedom to write.
Very few writers attain freedom
Through their works of art.
He is certainly one of these 'few'
Who dabble in art for soul's sake.

(Published in *The Asian Age*)

Love Requited

Twilight filters through
The glass window of Ivy Cottage
Overlooking the Himalayas.
'Come', says Ruskin, taking my hand,
'There's still light in my bedroom.'

Bina, his grandchild, a budding shutterbug,
Comes out running
From the interior
Responding to the call of his godfather
To snap both of us together.
The deed done
My heart brimful with gratitude
We sit at the drawing room-cum-library
For the last leg of the interview.

On the small courtyard
Just outside the entrance
Where the cypress proudly stands
A cricket match goes on,
The ball occasionally hitting
The door with a bang.
Ruskin looks unperturbed.

He has a divine way
To make peace with everything
However unpalatable.

Is there any Bond-enthusiast
Not aware of Sushila?
This finely fashioned character
Who features in time-stopping stories
On love by the author?

Consider the coda
Dedicated to her in *Roads to Mussoorie*;
Or the very recent *Funny Side Up*
Where Ruskin dotes on her yet again!
Not to forget 'Love is a Sad Song'
And 'Time Stops at Shamli'
Where she takes the centre stage.

Is the character real?
Is she aware of his fame? I ask.
'She knows!' muses Ruskin.
How? My interest gets the better of me.
'She phones me!' His voice sounds distant.
The emotion, the prime-mover
Behind all the stories on her,
Wells up in his serene eyes instantly.

Ages ago, writing on Ruskin's *contes d'amour*
One could never even imagine
One would fall in love oneself
With this lovely paramour!

Natasha the greatest female character
Ever created in world literature.
Is Sushila any less?

On Ruskin Bond

'One of my greatest regrets is that I have not met Ruskin Bond. There is so much I have read about him, and there is so much I have read about his work. Which is why my admiration for him grows—in the way he handles his simple themes, and the moving way he writes of the people and the place he knows so well. It all depicts a part of India that is virtually unknown to me, for I have never been that far north of the country. My residence has been in Orissa, and my poems have all happened from it. And often I have wished I could write as Ruskin does, so simply, instinctively and movingly. I suppose my poems are sorry because they miss the enchantment of Ruskin's prose.'

—Jayanta Mahapatra, the famous Indian English poet.

'Ruskin Bond is my guru. What can one say about one's guru? The greatest quality about him is that he is one of the humblest creatures that walked this earth. For someone who got success at the age of seventeen, and to have sustained that success in terms of publishing for about fifty years . . . it's just incredible. A lot of people work hard; only a few succeed. And one should always be grateful for the breaks that come one's way. That's what I have learnt from him. He is not only a writer's writer; he is also a great human being.'

—Ganesh Saili.

'Ruskin Bond has had a very tough struggle. He deserves every bit of success now. Uncomplainingly, he has been writing and writing and writing. Despite a very unhappy childhood, he persisted with his writing. As he says often, he has always been able to live on what small amount he earned which was not much. Small cheques of five hundred rupees used to be welcome for him. Now he is earning a lot, which he must never have dreamt of. Like in the old days, maybe even now, he lives a simple life.

'He is a very good writer because he never tries to impress you. He is really a natural writer. Words come to him just in the right place. And he's a very good human being. There is none who can say anything against him. He has never tried to hurt anybody. I will tell you a story.

'I have a friend of mine here who wanted very much to write a biography of Ruskin. This was before Ruskin's book (*Scenes from a Writer's Life*) came out. I said to my friend, "you can't write that!" But my friend said that Ruskin would never say that. Ruskin must have said to him very gently: "I'm already writing mine; or I would have loved you to write it." This is how Ruskin would say no. I think that's a very right picture of Ruskin.

'When my husband died, he wrote a very sweet letter to me. My husband was a great walker. He was a tall handsome man. He liked climbing hills which I didn't like. He would often go to Ruskin's place and spend hours with him. Ruskin was very sorry to hear it "because no longer would Brigadier Dalal be knocking at my door, trying to pursuade me to accompany him to the top of some hostile mountain".

'In the fifties, my short story "Sacrifice" won a world story competition. But they had not sent me a copy of the book in which the story appeared. At that time I think Ruskin must have just got the first prize for his maiden novel (*The Room on the Roof*). I remember I'd gone to buy rice from a shop whose owner was his foster mother. Bond was living upstairs there. She said to me in Hindi, "My son wants to meet you". I asked, "who is your son?" "Ruskin Bond", she said. I said, "I'd also like to meet him." Just then Ruskin came down the stairs with my book in his hand and asked if I had got the book. I said no. "I'll give it to you", he said. That's how we met first. He has been very helpful indeed.'

—Nergis Dalal, author.

Well-spring of Words

Mussoorie Writers' Festival – A Report

Mussoorie Writers' Festival Well-spring of Words

Shouldn't your writing feature ordinary people? What stops Bhasa literature from seeing the light of day? Why is the writer of today unable to draw upon his/her own mythical roots? Is there any way in which we can re-appropriate our cultural space and beat back offshoots of globalisation? Does the relationship between the writer and the publisher leave much to be desired?

These and many other issues were debated at the first Mussoorie International Writers' Festival, held at Woodstock, Landour, between 24-28 April 2007. The fest, which was sponsored by the Winterline Foundation, attracted a galaxy of writers from the United States of America (USA) and mostly from hometown Mussoorie and Delhi. The festival was also organised in special recognition of Ruskin Bond, 'our resident Wordsworth in prose'.

Amid incessant calls of cicada, a little way up from Hanifl Centre, venue for the inaugural ceremony, the principal of Woodstock School, Kaye Aoki, welcomed the participants sitting inside a makeshift tent, hoping that this sacred space would be a respite from the heat and dust of Delhi; and the act of knowing from each other would be stimulating and fantastic.

Chief guest, S.K. Das, chief secretary of Uttarakhand, recalled how in the midst of pushing files and doing demi-official correspondences, he would read Bond, Nehru and other writers with never-ending delight. He said that to him reading and writing was an antidote to the grind of day-to-day living, and rejuvenated the well-springs of creativity.

Speaking on writing across cultures, reputed author Nayantara Sahgal had the audience in thrall:

'I've run counter to this trend of migrant writing of cross cultures. I've always stayed put here in India. Neither God nor the cosmic bang is responsible for the creation of the world we live in. The West is still in charge. The empire is gone. But they're successful in making people believe that the world is a supermarket and the purpose of our life is to go shopping! I believe, no matter where you are located on the map, it gives you a special angle of vision. To me, home-grown sensibility is a priceless possession rather than the themes of exile and alienation of migrant culture. I hope for the day when national frontiers will disappear, and the writers will focus their attention more and more on those who are more sinned against than sinning.'

Talking about scholarly writing, psychoanalyst Sudhir Kakar recalled how original ideas were thought to be taken from sources not acknowledged. 'I've since emancipated myself from the accusations of my German professor. Scholarly discourses submerge the writer . . . We can only become what we are.'

The discussion took a somewhat vicious turn when Hugh Gantzer, travel writer, dropped the first bombshell by comparing the publishers as slightly worse than the dacoits in Chambal. Complaining about the royalty statement and distribution, he said whenever he wanted to speak to the publisher the answer was always the same – Sir! He is not on his seat! 'I have no time searching for his seat. We're in the business of searching for magic in ordinary people. . . .'

Sudhir Thapliyal took up the thread and said, 'Some bad writers are being published. It is bad editing, a lot of typos, all mixed up inside. It's not easy being a writer as far as money goes. Delhi is a terrible place, where nobody reads anything except classified advertisements! In book launches forum, the writer is not recognised, instead he is ignored. It's all about how much booze is consumed. Most Indian writers have never seen any money. . . .'

Later in the evening, there was a poetry reading session under the famed Lyre tree at Woodstock. Three poets—Erica Funkhouser, Ruskin Bond and Chris Sawyer-Laucanno—took part in it. It was the resident writer Ruskin who stole the show. He recited from his *Book of Verses* (Penguin, 2007) poems like 'The Demon Driver', 'Field Placings', 'We must love Someone', etc. He concluded with 'Lone Fox Dancing' for which he relied on his memory unlike other poets who preferred to read their poems from the books. In the banquet thrown in honour of Ruskin Bond that followed, Bond was awarded the first ever Poet Laureate of Landour Award. Anne Tofflemire entertained the audience with her endearing love songs. When I met renowned travel writer Bill Aitken after the session, he said, 'Ruskin is a poet. We're just pretenders.'

Udayan Mitra of Penguin, India, V.K. Karthika of Harper Collins and André Bernard of Guggenheim Foundation took up the issue with Hugh Gantzer and Sudhir Thapliyal the next day. Thapliyal was conspicuous by his absence. Both Udayan and Karthika spoke eloquently and never really crossed the threshold of decency despite being provoked.

What authors they choose and what they discard is their prerogative, say the publishers. The authors must carefully read their contract agreement, which the publishers scrupulously follow. 'The market governs us some way; but we have room to experiment. We receive too many unsolicited manuscripts, most of which remain under the slush pile. The biggest growth now is in general non-fiction,' they said. 'We respect our authors because they are the only persons we deal with.'

Responding to the accusation of Ashok Chatterjee, an eminent alumnus of Woodstock, that so much hype about a book and puerile interviews given by some authors take the reader for a ride, most of the authors agreed that such exposures actually help an author worth his/her salt to come into the limelight.

Later, a participant—who wished not to be named—opined that some participants misused the platform. They should not have gone public with such gripe against the publishers when they had got just one or two books published to their credit. Ruskin Bond struggled for years and years. But he never got vocal about all this.

Kirin Narayan, teacher and writer, while presenting her paper on 'Fiction, Folklore and Ethnography', touched the chord of the budding writers when she said:

'One should write about what one loves reading most. One should not use everything unless it helps the plot to move along. Writing is a long trek. All writers suffer loneliness. One shouldn't give up. One should not write for publication alone.'

On 26 April 2007, we went to Kaplani Village School run by Mussoorie Gramin Vikas Samiti. We drove along the Tehri road, along the Deodar Estate which was bought, Stephen Alter told me, by Patiala baron Ranbir Singh. The school is at the edge of a precipice. The students, on the cusp of their adolescence, welcomed us with Garhwali songs and dance. The main draw was Paro Anand who acted out a couple of stories with consummate skill; it had the children in stitches.

Among other things, Steve donated books by Paro Anand and Ruskin Bond translated into Hindi. Padmashri Sekhar Pathak spoke on the need to preserve forests to keep alive the age-old tradition and to prevent ecological disasters. As I listened to his address, I could see in the distance a clearing in the forest which was actually a helipad constructed for a minister.

Afterwards, on the same day, the discussion at the Roli Writers' Retreat at St. Asaph's, residence of Pramod Kapoor, publisher of Roli Books, started on a sombre note. Children's writer Paro Anand set the ball rolling with an account of her visit to Kashmir where she met unfortunate kids who had lost their parents in terrorist attacks. President Dr A.P.J. Abdul Kalam had once asked her, 'Why do you write about tragedy and unhappiness in stories meant for children?' 'How will I write another happy story again?', wondered Paro. She continued, 'What about horrific computer games like Road Rage in which you drive a car and every time you kill someone on the road you score points? There should be taboos in computer games rather than in children's literature! I don't leave a child absolutely hopeless. You can't always stick to safe ground. You've got to touch issues of contemporary interest.'

The discussion then turned to the question whether one should write in any language other than his/her mother tongue. Pavan K. Varma, director general of Indian Council for Cultural Relations (ICCR), diplomat and writer said, 'English still occupies a disproportionate cultural space because of colonial legacy. We're now far removed from our roots. There's a dumbing down of culture. In a book fair abroad, someone asked me, "Do you also write in English? It was like a slap on my face!" Talking about Hindi, he said, "It's a language of social exclusion. Hindi publishers are destitute. Why should that be? But it's heartening to note that the publishers who count are beginning to wake up and take notice of latest writing in regional languages."'

Pramod Kapoor lightened the atmosphere a bit by saying, 'Why hang on to a colonial hangover? English is very much our own language now. In any case, the Britishers now speak cockney, and we now speak English!'

On the afternoon of 27 April, the Parker Hall at Woodstock was packed to capacity to view the film *Blue Umbrella*, based on a story by Ruskin Bond of the same name. In the story, Binya happens to be the central character around whom everything else revolves. But in the film, one finds the role of Binya (played by Shreya Sharma) a little overshadowed by the shopkeeper Nandkishore (Pankaj Kapoor). Also, the episode of the umbrella toppling over the edge in a mild storm and how it is retrieved; then the chase given to Bijju by Binya and his brother, are all left out of the film. The songs are good; but the film as a whole could not live up to the magic of the story.

As soon as the film ended, the entire hall erupted into wild cheers. As Ruskin Bond and Vishal Bhardwaj took their seats on the podium, a barrage of questions flew up at them from students in the audience – Whether Bond and Vishal knew each other before the film was made; whether the story got fair treatment in the film; whether Bond ever knew that the story one day would be made into a film; whether the story is based on reality; how long did it take to shoot it. . . .

After the show was over, it was my turn to grill Bond closeted in his Ivy cottage!

A: *'You have just been awarded the first ever Poet Laureate of Landour award (2007). According to travel writer Bill Aitken, you're basically a poet. . . .'*

RB: 'I don't know, I was essentially a poet. Perhaps he is right. At the drop of a hat, I can still write a poem – anytime, anywhere. However, in order to earn, one had to write prose. It's so difficult to make money from poetry. Publishers don't make much out of it. Therefore, they're not keen to publish poetry.'

A: *'Now that recognition and honour is coming your way thick and fast, do you find time to reflect on the genesis of your career as a man of letters?'*

RB: 'Are they really coming thick and fast? Anyway I'm quite happy, particularly when I find my readership growing.

'Yes, of course, I often reflect on it. That was the best period of my writing. I enjoyed it the most. That was a period of glorious uncertainty. There was also the pleasure of the unexpected. Things would get published when I least expected it. At other times, you were unsure actually what the future held. It was unpredictable. I would not be sure from one month to the next how much I would earn and there were disappointments and rejections. . . .'

A: *'Were there repeated rejections?'*

RB: 'Yes! Very often; particularly with some of the early manuscripts. It was not easy to find a publisher abroad. In those days, for a book you had to look abroad for a publisher. Here you could publish shorter works in the magazines.'

A: *'Is there any manuscript still lying unpublished?'*

RB: 'Not now. But at that time, yes. For instance, *A Flight of Pigeons*, *Vagrants in the Valley*, and *Delhi Is Not Far* lay unattended at my desk for years.

'One practical reason why I took to writing children's books – they suited my preference for the shorter version of a novel. I found I'd got a gift for that, and I could also sell them abroad in seventies and eighties. *Blue Umbrella* was one of its kind published by Hamish Hamilton in England in 1972-73.'

A: *'Barring* Ek Tha Rusty *(TV serial),* Junoon *(film based on* A Flight of Pigeons*),* Blue Umbrella *(film produced by Vishal Bhardwaj), is there any other film based on your work?'*

RB: 'Another story is in the process of being filmed based on a part of *The Adventures of Rusty*. It's Sunil Advani from Bombay. He might have finished it by now.'

A: *'The film based on your story* Blue Umbrella*—how did the idea come about? Did Vishal Bhardwaj approach you?'*

RB: 'He phoned from Bombay; made me an offer. I said fine!'

A: *'Did he write the script himself?'*

RB: 'Yes.'

A: *'Did you have a look at that?'*

RB: 'Yes, he showed it to me.'

A: *'You okayed it?'*

RB: 'Right!'

A: *'Was there any minor change, any diversion from the main story?'*

RB: 'We talked about it a bit. He came and saw me a couple of times. There's a slight diversion. After all, you transfer the story to the visual medium. So there're bound to be certain aspects you'd stress more than others.'

A: *'That's perhaps the film-maker's prerogative. . . .'*

RB: 'Yes, yes, of course. He has basically kept to the story, the character and the theme, and he has expanded on it. He developed it a bit in his own way. Because he had to make a one-and-half-hour film. I'd say he's given more importance to one or two characters that might not have been that important in the book. . . .'

A: *'What about your experience in Goa when you saw the film for the first time?'*

RB: 'Well, I was going to a cinema hall after about twenty years. Mussoorie doesn't have any cinema hall any more. I had not been to one in Delhi for many many years. They put us right up in the front row. So I got stiff-necked and had a headache watching this huge screen in front of me. In the old days, the expensive seats were at the back. They gave us the honour, the privilege of being right in front of the screen. But if you remain at the back you get a better perspective.

'I enjoyed it. So did the audience. They also asked some questions afterwards. Vishal and I took questions from the audience on the film.'

A: '*Was there any snowfall during the shooting of the film?*'

RB: 'Yes, he made the film in Khajiar meadows near Dalhousie, very picturesque. They were doing it in winters. It began snowing, and snowing very heavily. So the last part of the film was filmed in snow. In the original story there's no snow. It happened during summers. The change didn't affect the story, it just made it more picturesque.'

A: '*Do you think that important meetings are always planned by the souls long before the bodies see each other?*'

RB: 'We often dream about what might be in the future. Maybe we don't interpret the dream correctly. I do think we can look ahead with the help of dreams. Also, it's possible to dream what you want to dream. That can tell you something about what lies ahead. You can also meet the sort of people you want to meet . . . Just today, there was a line in the paper which attracted my attention. It's a line from *The Alchemist* by Paulo Coelho. It says if you really want something—I'm paraphrasing it—and work towards it, the world will give it to you.'

A: '*Do you believe in that?*'

RB: 'If you really, really, truly want it, and you do work towards it, naturally, I think nine times out of ten, with the exception of accident and hammer of God or something. Maybe people don't want things enough. Or they want it too soon. . . .'

A: '*Is not your life ruled by too many surprises?*'

RB: 'I think there have been moments when something special came to pass which, perhaps, I'd not planned for. It could have been, as you say, an honour or an award. It could have been a particular story or a book doing better than I expected it to. Or, maybe, something from which I expected a lot but nothing happened. There were also chance meetings with interesting people.

'Of course, the tenor of my life hasn't changed much in that I've been living here up in the hills for the last forty years or more. There's a certain rhythm and regularity to life. Even so, things do happen from time to time which prevents it from becoming too monotonous.'

Reminiscence:
An Eternal Bond

An Eternal Bond

Subjects or ideas for articles, like in case of poems and stories, can pop up unexpectedly. If you are merged with your subject, it can be very inspiring. A sudden insight, if I may call it, into an event, which took place a few years ago, had my heart in thrall only the other day.

In January 2002, it was reported in *The Times of India* (Calcutta edition) that Padmashri Ruskin Bond, among other luminaries, had been invited to the Calcutta Book Fair, scheduled to be held form 30 January to 11 February 2002.

On the opening day of the fair, I got in touch with the fair organisers. 'He is expected to grace the occasion in the first week of February 2002,' an official told me. However, the subsequent digs at the Press Information Centre were met with some vague responses.

On entering the fair ground each day, my first job was to enquire about the exact date of Bond's arrival in the city of joy. I kept my ear cocked all the time for any announcement that might mention the name of the creator of the lovable rustic characters. There was no such announcement. A sense of despondency, I did not know how, crept into me as the fair progressed.

On 2 February, as I was rounding a corner tucked away from the hub of the fair, a bookshop from Bangalore caught my eyes. I would probably never have entered the shop if I had not met writer Anita Nair at her residence in Bangalore some time earlier.

I just felt an urge to ask the bookshop owner how the *Ladies Coupe* by Anita was doing.

My whole world consists of writers whose works I have emotionally identified myself with. Any prospects of either talking to or about the authors I love, immediately capture my subconscious, my soul in a way nothing else in the world can. So, I entered the Select Bookshop.

It was a kind of second hand bookshop. (They specialise in rare and antiquarian books with lithos, woodcuts and line drawings. They also undertake search services.) Searching through the stacks of books jostling for space in the crammed shop, I eyed a book – *Great Stories of the American West,* edited by Martin H Greenberg. Hoping to find a piece by Jack London in the anthology (I'm as enamoured of London as I'm of Bond), I opened the book with bated breath. Well, there was a story 'All Gold Canyon' by Jack London. What I liked most in the book was its 'author's section' in which were listed short profiles of writers like Jack London, Bret Harte, O. Henry, and Mark Twain, among others. As I held the book tight in my grip, I knew it would give me the license to launch into a conversation with the gentlemen manning the makeshift counter.

Yes, they were familiar with the works of Anita Nair. Talking about this and that, I suddenly heard myself asking Mr K.K.S. Murthy, owner of the Select Bookshop (71, Brigade Road Cross, Bangalore-560001) whether he knew anything about Ruskin Bond coming to the fair as a guest of honour to give away the prizes.

'We have no such information,' said Mr Murthy.

'A couple of weeks back, it was reported in *The Times of India*,' I said.

'Is that so? It'd indeed be great to have him with us,' said Mr Murthy. Mr Bond, he told me, had visited their bookshop in Bangalore not so long ago, stayed there for quite some time, and consented to be photographed. 'He's a very nice man you know,' he continued, 'If you happen to meet him at the fair this time, please tell him about our shop. We know he will certainly come again. You see we have his photograph.'

I bought the photograph and the book for a song. We shook hands. Mr Murthy came out of the shop and said, 'Please bring Mr Bond to our shop'. Another genuine lover of Bond, I thought. I nodded with my eyes going moist, and melted into the swelling crowd outside.

The remaining days of the fair, I kept my fingers crossed. There were gifted poet and writer Shiv K Kumar and other artistes. But the writer of my heart's choice was nowhere to be found. The fair came to an end leaving me in a state of despair.

It was only the other day it struck me that Bond perhaps responded, in his own silent and mysterious way (through his photograph taken at Bangalore), to my *crie du coeur* on 2 February (02/02/02) when destiny guided me to procure his photo from a stall that stood at the far corner of the ground, out of the prying eyes of the casual readers—a perfect ambience that solitude-loving Bond would have liked. Could it be that it was an instance of telepathy, I wonder now.

When I collected the photo, I was still hopeful that he would come, but eventually he did not. For reasons I shall never know. But this disappointment was necessary for me to realise that the direct communication of thoughts or feelings from one person to another without using speech, writing, or any other normal method, is possible.

Now I recall, with a frisson of ecstasy, how, on that day, I was gently led towards a particular stall—out of hundreds of such kind—at an obscure corner of the fair. There were quite a few other occasions when my sight was irresistibly drawn by an invisible power to a daily or a magazine carrying his writing or photograph.

How Bond reaches me, telepathically, particularly when I'm on a downer. If the 'insight' is real, then, perhaps, I too reach him once in a while!

(First published in *Garhwal Post*)